P9-BBT-854

YOUNG MUSIC MAKERS

Boyhoods of Famous Composers

YOUNG MUSIC MAKERS

Boyhoods of Famous Composers

by

Ireene Wicker

Illustrated by Jules Gotlieb

THE BOBBS-MERRILL COMPANY, INC.
A SUBSIDIARY OF HOWARD W. SAMS & CO., INC.
Publishers • INDIANAPOLIS • NEW YORK

Printed in the United States of America
Library of Congress Catalog Card Number: 61-14410

Contents

PART I. COMPOSERS OF EUROPE

PART II. COMPOSERS OF AMERICA

List of Illustrations

PART I
COMPOSERS OF EUROPE

JOHANN SEBASTIAN BACH

On the first day of spring in the year 1685, Johann Sebastian Bach was born in the town of Eisenach, Germany.

Even as long ago as 1685, there had been so many musicians in the family of Bach that the people there often called musicians "Bachs." There had been organists and music teachers in the family for generations. There were violinists and singers and makers of musical instruments. Even the Bachs who were not musicians by profession could play some instrument well, and sang in their church choirs.

So it was natural for the family to expect that another musician had been born with Johann Sebastian Bach.

He was a quiet, happy child. Since he was much younger than most of his brothers and sisters, he spent most of his time with his parents. He did not really miss playing with other children, for life with his parents meant music. And that was what Sebastian always wanted.

Many important events in his life took place in the spring of the year. The first of these was never forgotten by Sebastian. His father gave him a small violin when he was four years old. To the amazement of everyone in the family, he played it the first time he held it in his hands.

Then his father began to teach him all he could, and the little boy was excited and joyful. Now he would be able to join in the family music festival, held by the Bachs — all the Bachs — each summer. This time it was to be in Eisenach, at home.

Sebastian's older brothers and sisters were proud of the little boy, and were anxious for the visiting relatives to hear him play. But they were no more anxious than the child himself. Each day, when his father came home, Sebastian ran to him with his violin and asked for the lesson to begin.

"I cannot wait for our music festival this year," he said one day. "May I really play my violin with the rest of our family, Papa? And will they let me play some of my own music on it?"

"We shall see how it goes, my son," answered the father. "Let me hear you play, now."

Sebastian touched his bow to the strings and made the little violin sing.

His parents looked at each other proudly. Then an older brother, Jakob, came running in. He, too, listened in wonder and admiration.

"Bravo!" Jakob cried. "Sebastian will have to play for our festival this year."

"Yes, you are right, Jakob," the father agreed. "He will be the youngest Bach musician-composer at the festival."

That summer there were so many Bachs gathered together in Eisenach that the little house could hardly hold them. They sang for each other, and played for each other. Then they went up the mountainside to the ancient castle of the town. There they sang and played for all who wished to hear them.

After the big festival, Sebastian was allowed to stay up in the evenings whenever his parents and brothers and sisters made music together. As time went by, the youngest Bach seemed able to play any instrument and to invent melodies easily.

"I like to sing and play the music I hear in the air," Sebastian declared one night. "In the air, in the forest, in the church. In people's voices, too—in the crying and the laughing. And in the wind!"

His father laughed and said, "Well, Sebastian! Let us hear the music instead of speeches."

"All right, Papa. Here is the music of the forest."

Sebastian picked up his violin. He played a melody

that did seem to come from the sounds and rhythms of the forest.

Father Bach nodded. "Yes. It is a nice theme. Some day when you learn more about writing music, you must develop it, and others you have played. Soon I think you will be ready to study composition. I will start you with a book by the master musician, Buxtehude. You will enjoy that."

Sebastian's eyes were shining. He enjoyed everything he did, so he was sure he would like to study composition. "Everything is good!" he exclaimed. "Good and beautiful!"

It was a long time before he could say those words again. That spring, his mother and father were stricken during an epidemic, and within a very short time, both died.

The daughters of the family went to live with an older sister. Sebastian felt that his whole world had fallen apart when he and his brother Jakob were sent to another town, to live with their married brother Christoph.

Christoph Bach was also a musician, but he was very different from Sebastian's gentle, affectionate father. Also, he and his wife had children of their own. Two extra growing boys in his family meant a real burden, and Christoph was very cold and stern.

It was an unhappy spring for Sebastian. He needed

love and understanding and could find none. Frightened and lonely without his parents, he longed to pour his heart out in music. But he was never allowed to play the violin at all, or any of his own compositions on the clavier. He was to play only scales and exercises. Nothing was allowed in the way of games. In this stern household, months and then years went by.

One evening, as Sebastian sat at the clavier practicing, he remembered some of the melodies his father had told him to develop. Before he thought, he began to play one of them. How should he develop it? he wondered.

Suddenly Christoph strode angrily into the room.

"Sebastian! How often must I tell you to stop that ridiculous improvising? Play what is written!"

"I am not improvising, Brother Christoph," the boy said. "I am trying to develop a theme I composed long ago. Father suggested that I do so."

"Father indulged you far too much. Practice your scales now."

"Yes, Christoph."

Sebastian turned again to the clavier and to the scales he had practiced over and over again. He could play them better than Christoph himself. Now his eyes brightened and he looked hopefully at his older brother.

"Please, Christoph, when I have finished, may I play my violin tonight? I used to do it every night for Father and Mother. Please?"

When Sebastian saw the look on his brother's face, he bit his lips to keep back the tears.

"There!" exclaimed Christoph. "This is just what I mean! Always wanting your own way. When will you learn discipline? That, too, is important in music."

"Discipline—and love," murmured Sebastian under his breath.

"Silence! I am talking to you. You are not to play your violin at all. Play these scales for me now."

Sebastian sighed deeply. Dutifully, he played the scales. Tears filled his eyes, and he blinked hard to keep Christoph from seeing him cry.

He discovered that Christoph now possessed the book by Buxtehude which had been his father's—the book which could teach one how to write music. How he longed to study it! His father had wanted him to do so. Surely Christoph would let him have the book, he thought.

So he said to his brother, "Christoph, Father was giving me lessons in harmony and composition. He was about to begin with Buxtehude's book when—when he died. You know the book, Christoph. You have it here now. May I study it, as Father wished?"

Sebastian could not go on, but Christoph could, and did.

"Buxtehude's book, indeed! Nothing could be more ridiculous! That is too hard for you. You are far too young and untalented for such advanced study. You must rid yourself of the idea that you are a genius, Sebastian! You are an ordinary boy not yet twelve years old. You have much to learn and you will do as I say."

As Sebastian walked past the book shelves to go to bed, the volume by Buxtehude seemed to sparkle and shine in the moonlight. Sebastian turned to look again as he went out the door, and suddenly he had an idea.

"I could copy it," he thought, as he went slowly up the stairs. "When the moon shines the way it does tonight, I could see well enough without a light. Nobody would have to know, if I did it at night, without a candle, after everyone has gone to sleep. Would it be wrong, dear Father and Mother? Would it, dear God? I cannot believe that it would."

When the house was quiet and the moon was high in the sky, Sebastian crept down the stairs, softly, not making a sound. Yes, the moonlight still shone on the precious book. But the bookcase was locked, and Christoph had the key. The wooden bars of the shelves were far enough apart for Sebastian to reach through with his hand, but the books were too tightly packed in for him to wiggle out the treasured one.

The boy was about to give up his daring plan when he noticed that one of the wooden bars, close beside the book, was loose. Carefully he jiggled it. Out it came. In a moment the precious book was in his hands!

Joyously he carried it to the window. With the quill pen he used for his school work, and an unused copy book his father had given him, Sebastian Bach began to copy the musical text, note for note.

When the moonlight faded into darkness and Sebastian could see no more, he put the book in its place, carefully replaced the loose wooden bar and crept into bed, tired but happy.

For six long months, every moonlight night, Sebastian worked at his task. Sometimes he would be so tired he could hardly keep his eyes open. But he did not give up until he had finished copying the entire book. The night he did so, even the moon seemed to look smilingly down on the boy in the window.

But Sebastian was so tired he fell asleep before he had put the book away. He slept resting his head on both books. Christoph found him there next morning.

"So, Sebastian! It is just as I said. You have learned no discipline whatever! Even worse, you have deliberately disobeyed my orders. You shall learn to obey and you shall be punished until you do. You are never to see either one of these books again—the original which you took without my permission, or your copy of it."

Sebastian said quietly, "Brother Christoph, I did not wish to disobey you. I thought it could not be wrong for me to borrow the book, since Father had planned for me to study it."

Christoph's voice was cold. "You are living in my home now, Sebastian."

Sebastian nodded his head. "Yes, I know. You are right, of course. But — but it was beautiful music! And . . . even if I never see it again, it is mine, now. Because I remember every single note of it. I shall be able to play it, always."

"What are you saying?" Christoph looked scornful.

But his little brother answered firmly. "I am saying I have learned it now, as Father wished me to do. So I shall always be able to play it, or use what I have learned from it. That is what I am saying! And that is something you cannot take from me."

It was about this time that Sebastian's luck changed, and good things began to happen.

He was singing in the choir at the family's church, where the choirmaster took a great interest in him. This musician declared to Christoph that Sebastian was greatly gifted, quite possibly a genius.

"I shall do all that I can for the boy," the choirmaster said. "He must have the best musical training obtainable. The other church musicians feel as I do. Sebastian is remarkable—quite remarkable!"

From that moment on, Christoph never again stood in the way of his young brother's progress in music, even though he did not fully share the choirmaster's enthusiasm.

When Sebastian was twelve, it was decided that he should try for a place in the choir school of St. Michael's Church, in the town of Lüneburg. He was to go to Lüneburg with another boy. They would try out together, and, if they failed to win places in the school, they would return home together.

So twelve-year-old Sebastian Bach and his friend George Erdman started out together, on foot. There was no money for carriages or for stopping at inns. From Ohrdruff, their home, to Lüneburg was a two-hundred-mile journey over rough, hilly roads. But it was spring, and blossoms were beginning to brighten the forests and dingy fields. That helped to raise the spirits of the boys. Sometimes they were given a ride in a farmer's cart. Often they slept in a loft or on beds of pine needles under sheltering trees.

At last they arrived in Lüneburg and set out to look for the choir school. There it was, near the church, an ancient building with a red brick tower. When the two tired young boys appeared at the door and announced that they had walked nearly all of the miles from Ohrdruff, they were welcomed with warmth and kindness.

Sebastian and George were only too glad to rest, to eat, to wash and change their clothing at last. The next morning, they found their own clothes clean and waiting beside their cots. Gratefully, they dressed and presented themselves to the director to try out for the choir school.

The director looked at the boys thoughtfully, and smiled encouragingly.

"You are both to be congratulated," he said. "I only hope that you are qualified for the positions you have so bravely come here to find. The only qualities that count when we select boys for the choir are character and the ability to sing—to sing very well indeed, if you would belong to the choir of St. Michael's."

Sebastian nodded solemnly. When the music was given to him, he sang with such joy and read the music so expertly that the choirmaster embraced him.

"Yes, yes," said the choirmaster, "you know music! You *are* music, my boy. Your voice will lift up the choir."

George Erdman, too, was accepted, and so a good new life began for the two boys. They were to live in the church school, to have lessons on the various instruments, to take part in all the musical activities of St. Michael's, as well as do regular school work.

To Sebastian Bach, it was the happiest time of his life since before he had lost his beloved parents. Here, as at home in Eisenach, the world was music. There was a library filled with music books which he could study to his heart's content. He could play what he wished when practice hours were over and lessons were finished. He could learn to play all the instruments for which there was time. Best of all, he could play his violin whenever he wished.

The choirmaster watched him with great interest and growing excitement. One day as he saw Sebastian sit down at the clavier, he said to him, "Sebastian, you already play the clavier beautifully. Why not have a try at the organ in the church today?"

"Maestro! You mean I have permission? That is wonderful!"

The boy ran to the loft like the wind. He sat reverently at the big church organ. Instinctively, he touched the wooden foot pedals and explored the rows of keys with his fingers. He began to play, improvising melodies which resounded through the church in beautiful tones.

Thus did Johann Sebastian Bach discover the greatest joy of music for him—playing the organ. From the very beginning, he composed music especially for the organ, music that will live as long as there are people on earth to hear it.

Sometimes while Sebastian was in the choir school in Lüneburg, he saw his cousin, Maria Bach. She understood his need for music. They were good friends and often confided their dreams and hopes to each other. One day Sebastian told Maria how much he wanted to go to Lübeck to hear the great Buxtehude play the organ.

"Oh, yes," Maria said, "Buxtehude! Isn't he the master whose book you copied, in the moonlight?"

Sebastian nodded with a little smile. "Yes, Maria. Poor Christoph. He was very angry. He thought I was so foolish. He would think me even more so if he knew I wanted to go three hundred miles just to hear Buxtehude play. I suppose it is too far and would keep me away from my work here too long. It would not be fair to the choir school."

"No, I suppose not," Maria agreed. "But, Sebastian, there is a fine organist in Hamburg. Reinken—is that not his name?"

"Reinken, yes," Sebastian said. "I know he plays in Hamburg."

"Well, you might go there, Sebastian. It would help in your own playing. And your choirmaster at school might think it is a good idea. Hamburg is not so far."

Sebastian was pleased with that idea. Hamburg was only thirty miles away.

"I could walk and be there in good time if I started early in the morning," he said. "It's a wonderful plan, Maria. I'll go tomorrow, if Maestro says I may."

Sebastian did exactly that. He walked the thirty miles to Hamburg one day, and thirty back, the next.

Tired but happy after his long journey, he sat down for a moment on the bench in front of the inn where Maria worked. Maria ran outside and sat down beside her cousin.

"Did you go, Sebastian? You look so tired. You must have walked all the way. Come inside and have something to eat."

"Thank you, Maria, but I can't. I spent what money I had in Hamburg."

"Please, Sebastian, let me lend you some. If not, the innkeeper is very kind. He would be glad to give you your supper."

Sebastian was too proud for that. He said, "I

wouldn't think of such a thing! Anyway, I am not hungry, not a bit. Just tired. Thank you, Maria."

Then the girl ran to the innkeeper. "Please, sir," she said, "can you help me? My cousin has walked all the way to Hamburg and back, without enough to eat, I know. Just so he could hear some organ music! I would like to give him some money, but he refuses to take it. What can I do? He must eat!"

"Hmmm," said the innkeeper. "I have an idea. There used to be a rich old fellow who lived here. He would watch out the window, and when he saw someone who looked tired or hungry, he would throw a coin or two down to the road. The traveler would pick it up and, nine times out of ten, come in and eat his first good meal in days. Let's try that trick!"

"Oh, yes, sir!" Maria laughed happily and ran to get some coins. She dropped them from an upstairs window to the ground at Sebastian's feet, and watched to see what would happen.

Sebastian picked up the coins, looked at them curiously, and jumped so high he almost bumped his head on the innkeeper's sign.

"Maria!" he shouted. "Maria, look! What wonderful luck! Money fell from the sky like manna from heaven."

"How wonderful, Sebastian," cried Maria, running outside again. "Now you can come in and eat."

"Eat!" Sebastian looked at Maria as if she were joking. "Did you say *eat?* Oh no, Maria! How could I waste these precious coins on food? Reinken is going to play in Hamburg again tonight. I was longing to hear him. Now I can! Good-by, Maria dear. You have brought me good luck."

And as Maria stood there speechless, Sebastian kissed her soundly on both cheeks, threw his cap into the air, caught it happily and started off as though he had rested for a week.

Maria went inside to tell the innkeeper what had happened. He too was looking up the road, scarcely able to believe what he saw.

"Whatever will happen to him?" asked Maria.

"Only something good," answered the innkeeper slowly. "When anyone loves life and music that much, only something good."

Those long walks of Johann Sebastian Bach were the first of many others. He did walk to Lübeck to hear Buxtehude, later on—when he lived a little closer to Lübeck! All his life he thought nothing of walking miles for music he could hear in no other way.

Shortly after the two trips to Hamburg, Sebastian was offered a place in the court orchestra of the Duke of Weimar. He was on his own at last in the world of music, though he was still only a boy in his teens.

A little later, he became church organist in the town of Arnstadt. Maria went with him to hear him practice for his first Easter services there. As she listened, she tried to think what music Sebastian was playing.

"What is it?" she asked at last. "It is so beautiful. Such lovely music for Easter! Surely I should know it, but I cannot seem to place it."

"No wonder, Maria, since it was never played before," said Sebastian. He was pleased with Maria's understanding and knowledge of music. But then, of course, she was a Bach! "It is a melody that came to me just now, when I began thinking of music for Easter."

"It makes me feel like singing," Maria said softly. "The words of St. Matthew would be good for it."

Sebastian had been thinking of the same thing. The Easter story in the Bible, told by St. Matthew, seemed to him so wonderful that he must write music to accompany it.

"Sing then, as I play, Maria."

Maria sang some of the words she knew, fitting them to Sebastian's music.

That was the beginning of Bach's *St. Matthew Passion*, which is sung at Eastertime still.

Neither Sebastian nor his cousin noticed anyone enter the church while they were playing and singing. As the last chord of music faded into silence, a stern voice rang out harshly.

"What is going on here?"

It was the Deacon of the church who spoke. He was angry and shocked. Maria looked frightened. Sebastian stood up and bowed politely.

"Sir, I was trying out some new music I have written, and——" The church official cut him short. "Herr Bach, your ideas of music are ridiculous! The music we have used for two hundred years is not good enough for you? And now you bring a strange maiden into the sacred halls of the Holy Church, right before the Easter services! I shall report this to the Elders and see that you are dismissed at once."

Before Sebastian could answer, a gentleman stepped forward from the shadows and addressed the angry Deacon.

"I beg your pardon, Deacon, but I must speak. This morning I was walking in the village, when suddenly I heard this beautiful music and could not resist stepping inside the church. I would not have missed it for anything."

Before the stranger could go on, the Deacon interrupted him.

"Humph! The young man's behavior is inexcusable!"

"I cannot agree with you, sir," said the stranger

emphatically. "His music will rank with the finest in the world. You had better think well before criticizing him, for he is a genius. And furthermore, he ——"

"*You* are an expert, I suppose?" snapped the Deacon.

"I am considered so by some," answered the stranger quietly. "My name is Buxtehude."

Sebastian and Maria gasped. Sebastian looked more closely at this stranger who was defending him. Yes! It was the great Buxtehude, whom he had recently seen in Lübeck. He could not contain his excitement.

"Sir!" he exclaimed. "Maestro! I heard you play in Lübeck last month. It was wonderful. Your writing on music has meant much to me, too. Once I copied every note in your book of harmony and composition. All my life I have longed to meet you. You are a great master!"

"Thank you, my boy," said Buxtehude with pleasure. "Now, that music you were playing—tell me about it."

"Well, sir, it was music that came to me as I thought of St. Matthew's Easter story. The same thought occurred to my cousin, Maria, here—so perhaps it is right. The music, for St. Matthew's gospel, I mean."

"It is right, Herr Bach," the famous musician

assured him. "You must not fail to write it out. It is very beautiful, also. So beautiful that I think it will someday be heard all over the world, at Eastertime."

The Deacon looked on in wonder as the great Buxtehude bowed before young Sebastian Bach.

Sebastian and Maria were married, later on. Sebastian became a happy, hard-working man, and spent his life as an organist, teacher and composer. The list of his compositions is almost endless. His music—especially his music for organ and for a choir of voices—is admired by all the world.

He became the greatest in the musical family of Bach, and one of the greatest composers of all time. Some people think him the king of all musician-composers. His music has given beauty and joy to the world for more than two hundred years.

WOLFGANG AMADEUS MOZART

Suppose you tried to compose a sonata without any music lessons—or even tried to read this book without having learned to read. Could you do it? Unless you are a genius, you would not know how to begin.

Wolfgang Amadeus Mozart was a musical genius, such a great one that he knew how to compose music before he was taught. When he was three years old, he could play melodies he had heard only once, and create music he had never heard. The first time he sat at a harpsichord, held a violin in his hand, or touched the keys of an organ, he played as though he had had many lessons on the instrument. It was as easy and natural for him to do these things as it is for most children to begin to crawl, or to laugh and cry.

Mozart had the gift of true pitch. That is, he could name the tone of any sound he heard, or of any note struck at random on a musical instrument.

Other great musician-composers have had some of these gifts, or a little of all of them. But none was so richly gifted as Mozart.

In his short lifetime, Mozart composed more music of every different kind than any other composer. Operas, symphonies, solo pieces for many different instruments; church music; chamber music for small groups of string instruments; songs for children, and for famous singers. The list goes on and on.

It is strange and very sad that this great genius was appreciated and applauded only during his childhood. He was a very famous child, because of his music. But when he grew up, he could not even make a living with that music.

His childhood began in a story-book world, more than two hundred years ago. He was born in the city of Salzburg, Austria, on January 27, 1756. Standing in the Alps Mountains, Salzburg is a beautiful and historic city. The towers of its fortress and its cathedral rise above the rest of the city, and look like a picture in a fairy tale.

Little Wolfgang Mozart seemed like a story-book child, too. He was handsome and cheerful. He had a pretty, older sister, a handsome, talented father, and a beautiful mother. The whole family had a good time together, and Wolfgang was surrounded by music from the day he was born.

His father was a musician at the Court of the Archbishop, there in Salzburg. He taught music, played the harpsichord and violin, and was named Court Composer when Wolfgang was a baby.

Whenever the father, Leopold Mozart, played at home, or practiced there with other members of the Archbishop's orchestra, the little boy and his sister Marianne listened. They were always quiet and happy as long as there was music.

One December evening, when Wolfgang was three years old, there was excitement at home. It was Papa Mozart's birthday. Wolfgang and Marianne ran back and forth from kitchen to parlor, helping their mother with a surprise celebration for Papa.

Every time Wolfgang went to the parlor, he looked eagerly out the window. At last he shouted at the top of his voice:

"He's coming! Papa's coming! Mama, hurry, hurry! I hear him coming up the steps. . . . Oh, he is here! Happy birthday, Papa, happy birthday!"

After the celebration dinner, Leopold Mozart played the music his children begged for. First the violin, then the harpsichord. As he played, he noticed how Wolfgang watched every movement of his fingers and clapped his own little hands with each beat of the music. The child was keeping perfect time and smiling joyfully.

Papa Mozart stopped playing and took the little boy on his knees. "Now, Wolfgang, what makes you smile so? Is it the music? Do you like it so much?"

"Yes, Papa. I like it more than anything. I like to hear it all the time. I do, too, even when you are not playing."

"How can you do that, child?" the father asked.

"It is easy, Papa. I close my eyes and remember the sound. Some day I will be a musician, too. Teach me to play the harpsichord, Papa? Teach me right now?"

Papa Mozart threw back his head and laughed heartily. "You, Wolfgang? Ach! Bübchen! My little boy! You are far too small. You could not stretch those tiny fingers to play an octave of big white keys. You could not reach up to the keys at all, without putting pillows and big books on the bench. And what about those little short legs? You could not touch the pedals of the harpsichord. No, Bübchen, you will have to grow a few more inches."

Then he looked at his daughter. "But Marianne, ah, that is different," he said. "Marianne is seven years old, now, and I think it is time she learned to play."

Marianne was pleased. "You did promise to teach me, Papa, a long time ago."

So then and there, Marianne had her first lesson on the harpsichord. Papa Mozart showed her how to sit up straight on the bench, and how to hold her hands. He helped her strike the keys in the right way, lightly, without pounding. He gave her a little piece to try, a minuet he had written himself.

After an hour Marianne could play the simple music quite well, and her father was pleased. Neither of them noticed that Wolfgang carefully watched and listened.

When Marianne's lesson was over, the little boy climbed up to the bench in front of the harpsichord. Then he played the music he had just heard, and he played it perfectly.

His father and mother looked at him in amazement. Papa Mozart was beaming with excitement.

"Well, little Bübchen! Bravo! This is indeed a happy day! Even though you prove your Papa to be wrong! You show me that you can play the harpsichord, three years old or not! Well, you shall both have lessons in music every day, from now on!"

So the study of music began for the Mozart children. They were taught daily with great care and skill by their gifted father. Often he wrote minuets, which Marianne learned in a few days of practicing.

Wolfgang could always play the pieces correctly after hearing them once.

"I did not know such a thing could be!" said Frau Mozart.

"Nor I," agreed her husband. "Never have I seen anything like it. He seems to know everything before he is taught, and to play well without any effort. His memory is fantastic, and his ear is faultless! It is indeed a miracle. He even plays original melodies."

The father proudly began to keep a notebook of Wolfgang's original pieces. He wrote the music down as he watched the boy play it, and soon the book was full.

"The music is good, too," said Papa Mozart. "And the form is always correct. It is as if the boy had studied composition!"

When Wolfgang was about five years old, he was no longer satisfied to let his father write down his music. He wanted to do it himself. So he began to try writing his own manuscripts. Only Marianne knew about this at first, because Wolfgang was not very proud of all the ink blots and smudges he made on the paper.

One day, Marianne looked at him with a puzzled frown on her pretty face.

"Wolfgang, how do you do it? How can you write

music when you have not yet learned how to write words?"

"I can do it because I have to do it. It is in here and I have to get it out!"

"In where?" asked Marianne, wonderingly.

"Here," said Wolfgang solemnly, touching his head. "I have to write it down to get it out of my head. To make room for the music that comes along to fill up my head again! Now," he said, "I am going to write out some pieces I have already composed, and I am going to give them to Papa when we have his next birthday celebration. Here is one of them. Shall I play it for you?"

"Oh, yes," said Marianne. "Please do."

As she listened, her eyes grew rounder and bigger. She hugged her little brother and kissed him.

"Wolfgang! It is beautiful. You must play it for Papa when he gets home tonight."

When Leopold Mozart came home, he saw his five-year-old struggling with a pen and sheets of music paper.

"What? Writing!" Papa said. "Let me see." He looked over Wolfgang's shoulder.

"It is a sonata for your birthday, Papa. But it is not quite finished," the little boy said as he wrote. "There! I am sorry there are so many blots. I drop ink, and the pen sticks, too. I don't know why."

His father smiled. "Well, perhaps it is because you have not been using a pen very long. Ah! I see you have written the notes over the blots well enough for a good musician to follow them."

He read Wolfgang's sonata carefully. He was smiling and shaking his head at the same time.

"Bübchen, this is a very beautiful sonata," he said. "And in spite of the ink blots and smudges, it is written out quite correctly. But there is one thing that worries me . . ."

"Oh, Papa," cried Wolfgang, with a long face, "what is it? What is wrong?"

"Nothing is wrong with the music at all," said his father, with a twinkle in his eyes. "But it is much too hard to play, at least for most musicians."

"Oh, is that all!" said little Wolfgang. "Sonatas are always hard to play well, even the simple ones. You know that! They have to be practiced first. But this one is not too hard. I will show you!"

He hurried to the harpsichord to play his music for his father. The little sonata *was* beautiful, singing and gay and full of melody. It is still played often, today.

A good friend of Leopold Mozart's came to practice with him that evening, and visit with the family afterward. When the visitor heard Wolfgang play, and saw the music he had written, he was amazed.

"I would not believe this if I did not hear it with my own ears and see with my own eyes," he said. "You know, I think that Wolfgang is more than a very nice little boy—more than a good son and a loving brother. I think he is also the Spirit of Music, and he is playing a joke on all of us. The Spirit of Music is only pretending to be a little boy, so that he can live in this charming and gifted family and have a good time with them!"

It was a happy evening for all of them. So Wolfgang was surprised, later on, at something Marianne said.

The lights were out and they were about to go to sleep, when she whispered anxiously, "Wolfgang, Papa is worried."

The little boy thought that was a silly idea. How could it be true? "Worried? But Papa was laughing and happy all evening," he said. "We had such a good time."

"I *know,*" Marianne said. "But that does not mean anything. I heard Papa tell Mama that even with his new job as Court Composer, he is very worried about money. It costs money, Wolfgang, to buy shoes and books and medicine and so many things!"

Tender-hearted little Wolfgang was wide awake at once. He sat up in bed and said to Marianne in a loud whisper: "Then we must help."

"Oh, Wolfgang, how could we help? Unless we stopped eating, and wearing shoes."

"Silly! We could not do that. If we stopped eating, we would be sick. And if we stopped wearing shoes, we could not travel, and that would spoil our plan."

"Oh, you say the funniest things! What plan?"

"Our plan to help Papa."

"Oh! Of course. We have a plan, Herr Wolfgang," said Marianne with a giggle. "Let me see now . . . I seem to forget. Just what was our plan, Herr Mozart?"

"Goodness, Fräulein Mozart!" said Wolfgang, in the tone of His Majesty, the Emperor. "My goodness, but you are forgetful, child! Our plan is to travel and give concerts together, like other musicians!"

"Wolfgang!" Marianne was frightened at the very thought of such a thing. "How could we? How do you know Papa would want us to do anything like that? What makes you think the Archbishop would let him leave Salzburg for such a reason? You are much too young to understand all the different problems——"

"I am five-and-one-half years old!" said Wolfgang stoutly. He jumped out of bed and stood on tiptoe to show how tall he had grown.

"And besides, I have studied music all my life, and written it, too! I can play the harpsichord and the violin and I can sing. You can sing and play the harpsichord. And we can play duets together, too, if we practice."

"Duets?" asked Marianne. "What kind of musical instrument is a duet? You see? You don't know."

"I do," said Wolfgang quickly. "You are the one who doesn't know. I know, because I made up some for us to play. We both play the harpsichord at the same time together. You play the bass notes and I play the treble notes. Marianne, I have written some music for duets! Let's go to the parlor—I'll show it to you."

Marianne was interested now. Quietly she led the way from the dark bedroom. Softly the children tiptoed to the harpsichord in the still-bright parlor. Voices came from the kitchen, but Wolfgang and Marianne thought only of the music.

Wolfgang brought one of his smudgy sheets of paper to his sister. She studied it a moment, then she tried a few chords. The boy joined in with the treble part, which had more than twice as many notes as hers and was much harder to play.

Papa Mozart came hurrying into the parlor to see what was going on. He stood there, spellbound. The music that he heard was unusual and exciting.

By the time the children finished their duet, their mother was listening, too.

"Bravo!" said Papa. "A sonata for four hands instead of two. And a very good one, too."

"It will sound better after we practice it," said Wolfgang. "This is the first time we ever played it. Marianne had lots of ink blots on her part. So did I, but I wrote the notes in the first place, so I knew what they were! We thought a duet would make our concerts more interesting."

"What concerts?" asked Papa and Mama Mozart, making another duet.

Everybody laughed and Wolfgang ran to kiss his father.

"Papa, Marianne told me you are worried about money. I thought if we practice and work very hard, we could play some concerts. Then we could earn a little extra money for you."

Papa and Mama Mozart looked at their children in amazement. Then they looked at each other, thoughtfully. This idea of Wolfgang's was not a bad idea, at all.

The children really were musicians—Marianne was quite good for a child, and Wolfgang, of course, was a genius! Their ages, their music, their charm, everything would attract listeners. They would not have stage-fright, as some children might, for they loved to play, and they had already performed for small audiences of the family friends.

Wolfgang had even performed once in a great concert hall, playing with the court orchestra. And how the audience had cheered! The boy was very young, of course, for a concert tour. But musically, he was quite ready. He was born ready for anything in music.

"Yes," said Leopold Mozart to his wife and the eager children. "I think it may work out, this concert idea of yours. I will ask the Archbishop for permission to be away from court for a while."

It was not long before he came home from work one day to announce that the permission was granted. "Now we must make arrangements for our tour," he said. "I think we will start in January. And I think we will be invited to play before many important people, in many countries. That is what I think of my wonderful children!"

Marianne and Wolfgang and their father left Salzburg two months from that day. Their tour was a happy, exciting time for all of them. They played in the courts of Austria, Germany, France, England, Belgium and Holland. They played before the Pope in the Vatican, and in many cities of Italy.

Everywhere, their audiences loved them. Wolfgang had more than his share of attention and applause, because he was so young and already such a brilliant performer and composer. But Marianne did not mind. She was proud of her little brother, and loved him very much.

When the children played for the Royal Court of Austria, a funny thing happened. Wolfgang ran to the Empress to thank her for her kindness and applause. He reached up, put his arms around her neck, and kissed her. Then as he turned to go, he slipped on the marble floor and fell over the long sword he had to wear at court. Down he went on that hard floor, and then he cried like any little boy.

The Emperor's daughter, Marie Antoinette, ran to him quickly. She helped him up and gave him a hug and kiss, "To stop the hurt," she said.

The princess was only a year older than Wolfgang and he thought that he liked her very much. "Thank you, with all my heart," he said gratefully. "When I grow up I will marry you!"

There were other concert tours in the years of Wolfgang's childhood. Sometimes he played with Marianne, and sometimes he appeared alone. Everywhere he was a great success. Everyone took a special interest in him and his compositions.

All the time, he never stopped composing. He learned to use the pen much better, and not to make blots on his music paper. He wrote songs, sonatas, symphonies. When he was only eleven years old he wrote his first opera. It was produced many times, with great success.

Many honors came to Wolfgang in these happy years. He was made a Cavalier and Knight of the Golden Cross by the Pope. The great Italian city of Bologne elected him a member of its Philharmonic Academy, an honor never before given to anyone so young.

But the fairy-tale childhood came to an end. Mozart's young manhood was filled with disappointments. He wrote and wrote, composing more and more beautiful music, but he received very little appreciation.

Often he was neglected, or treated unfairly and even cruelly. Yet he never became bitter or resentful. His happy, loving nature did not change. The music that filled his life also filled his heart. There was no room left for thoughts of meanness, revenge or bitterness.

His last opera, *The Magic Flute,* was written when Mozart was ill and weak, poor and low in spirit. But it sparkles with wit and gaiety. It is as joyous an opera as you will ever hear.

Mozart's music is proof that the quality of genius cannot be hurt by the world's neglect. And today the world is very fortunate indeed to have the beauty given it by Wolfgang Amadeus Mozart. We are also very fortunate to have so much of this great composer's music on phonograph records and available to the majority of people.

LUDWIG VAN BEETHOVEN

Bonn is a beautiful city on the banks of the Rhine River, in Germany. In 1770, it was a busy river port with sailboats carrying passengers and freight from one town to another, fishermen coming and going with their day's catch, barges being towed back and forth and all kinds of river-boat traffic with its hurrying, scurrying noise and bustle.

On the seventeenth of December, 1770, one of the arrivals on the old ferry was a musician named Beethoven. He played in the band at the court of a German prince—the Elector of Cologne. Herr Beethoven was a lively little man dressed in a tricorn hat, flaring knee-length coat and knickers. His dark eyes flashed, and his wig, tied in back with a black bow, in the custom of the times, bounced up and down as he hurried over the rough cobblestones.

He did not stop until he reached a tall old tenement house. Then he opened the gate, ran into the dark hall and fairly flew up the stairs to the small apartment at the top of the building.

"Where is my grandson?" he shouted. "Eh? Let me see my grandson! Where is the new member of the Beethoven family?"

He beamed happily at his daughter-in-law, and gazed intently at the tiny baby in her arms. The baby twisted up its face and began to cry.

"La, la, la! Listen to the strength of the lungs! Only a musician could cry like that," Grandfather said. "And his name, Maria? What is it to be?"

"His grandfather's name." Maria smiled affectionately at the proud musician as he admired his grandchild. "His name is to be Ludwig, after you. And we want you to go with his father for the christening."

So a new Ludwig van Beethoven was baptized the morning of December 17, 1770. Proudly Grandfather Ludwig looked on, and then took the baby in his arms. That was the beginning of a warm, happy companionship for the two Ludwigs.

Every moment he was not busy with the orchestra, the choir, or his music pupils, Grandfather came to play and sing with baby Ludwig. From the time he could walk, the little boy went across the narrow street to his grandfather's house. He went early in the morning and stayed most of the day.

"Breakfast, Grandpa?" Ludwig would ask eagerly. "And then music?"

Grandfather was pleased at the boy's interest in music. He began to teach him when little Ludwig was very small. Other musicians often came to Grandfather's house to play, so the boy could hear all the music he wanted. He heard singing, violin, pianoforte, and all the instruments of the band.

In his own home he heard music, too. Johann, little Ludwig's father, was a singer and violinist. Like everyone else, the father took it for granted that the child would grow up to be a musician, too.

When Ludwig was just three, his grandfather died. There were no more long happy days of music with him, no more walks in the woods and fields outside the city or along the riverbank. The little boy missed his grandfather very much. But he still had music.

He wanted to play and sing as his grandfather had done, and to play the violin as did his father. So he was glad when his father said, "Ludwig, we will start music lessons in earnest now. It is time you learned. You are old enough now."

The little boy was not yet four years old!

Father Johann was very stern about the lessons. He insisted that Ludwig must practice many hours a day. And he must practice exercises and scales, not singing melodies.

Ludwig began to dislike the music lessons with the father. Sometimes he even wept with anger over them. If he could not play beautiful music instead of exercises, he would rather play out of doors with other children.

Sometimes, when his father was not listening, the boy would play whatever melody came into his head. Music of his dreams, he called it.

When Father Beethoven discovered Ludwig doing this, he was angry.

"Stop the foolishness, Ludwig! You must keep at the scales and the exercises. You will not be a good pianist unless your fingers are strong and can fly over the keys. You must learn to play properly. That is technique, and technique you must have. That is the most important thing in learning music. Not dreams!"

"Yes, father," said Ludwig obediently. But he was angry, too.

After his father left for choir practice, Ludwig grumbled, "If I could play music I dream about, just once in a while—But no! Scales, scales, scales!"

He looked up to see his mother smiling at him. He always felt very close to his mother, and told her his troubles and dreams.

"Mama, *what* shall I do? What *can* I do?"

His mother said gently, "Do just as you are doing,

Ludwig. Try to practice as your father wants you to, and please try to be patient. Father is really proud of you. He is proud of your talent."

"Then why won't he let me make real music?" Ludwig banged on the keys.

"He has many worries, dear, many troubles. Money is the cause of most of them. We never have enough money for all our needs, to buy enough wood to feed our fire or enough food to feed our bodies. So perhaps your father feels you will be able to help out soon, if you learn to play well, very quickly. Perhaps he hopes that you will be able to play a concert now and then."

"A concert!" Ludwig smiled, thinking of the music he would play in a concert. No exercises! "I will do my best and learn everything I can as quickly as possible," he thought.

If he could learn to play well enough to give a concert, he might have a chance to go to Vienna. The "City of Music," Vienna was called. Many great composers and performers lived there. Some were teachers, too. If he could study in Vienna, he might even enjoy practicing scales.

So Ludwig worked harder than ever, with his father as teacher, and cheerfully did his best. He played in a concert when he was seven. Soon after that, he got a new teacher, by a happy accident.

The Beethovens had moved to a small house with rooms on the street floor. One spring evening, Ludwig was practicing with the doors and windows open. From scales and exercises, he began to play some melodies of his own. Suddenly, a cheerful-looking stranger appeared at the window and began to applaud.

"Very nice, Baby Maestro. Very nice, indeed. Bravo!"

"Thank you, sir," said Ludwig. "My name is Ludwig Beethoven. Who are you?"

"I am a nobody," said the stranger. "Only Tobias Pfeiffer, a poor musician without a home. I have just arrived in Bonn to sing in your beautiful opera house."

Ludwig smiled. He had heard of Herr Pfeiffer, the new opera star.

Tobias Pfeiffer said, "Now, I was just thinking as I heard you play. I have long taught music. I would like to teach a fine young musician like you, Ludwig Beethoven. I would also like a place to live! Now I wonder . . . Could I stay here, in your home, and give you lessons to pay for my lodging?"

"Wait, sir, if you please," said the boy. "I shall ask my father."

"That will not be necessary," said Johann from across the room. He had come in, and overheard Herr

Pfeiffer's words. In his gruff, stern way, he was pleased.

"We shall try out this plan," he said. "From what I have heard, Heff Pfeiffer is a good musician. Perhaps he can improve your work in the writing of music. You must learn theory, harmony, all the things a composer must know."

Herr Pfeiffer bowed very low. He saw at a glance how stern the father was and how eager the boy was to please him.

After Johann had gone, Herr Pfeiffer bowed again to Ludwig and said with great warmth, "Ludwig Beethoven, I am delighted."

Ludwig replied with a lift of his spirits and a feeling of excitement. "Thank you, Professor. I am glad also, very glad."

"That is good, little Maestro," said Herr Pfeiffer gaily. "Then let us begin at once. First of all, let me hear you improvise."

Ludwig's eyes shone. Imagine being asked to improvise!

"My father does not like me to do so," he told his new teacher. "But I do. Music rings in my ears, all the time, and I want to play it—my *own* music—all the time, some day."

Then he played for Herr Pfeiffer a lovely melody of his own making. He sang softly as he improvised.

Professor Pfeiffer was silent for a moment after Ludwig had played. Slowly he nodded his head. Then he spoke gently to the eager little boy with the bright black eyes.

"Ludwig, as I listen to you play, I am very sure that your dreams will come true."

Ludwig studied with cheerful, gifted Tobias Pfeiffer for a year. Herr Pfeiffer understood the child, liked him, and gave him confidence. There was little time for anything but music in his life now. Lessons on the pianoforte and the violin. Hours of practice on these instruments. Lessons in composition, and hours of study for these lessons. Months and years went by in this way.

When Ludwig was only nine, he made his first concert tour. He went to Holland, a land his grandfather had often told him about. The Beethoven family had originally come from Holland, so young Ludwig was especially happy to perform there.

Later, when Ludwig was eleven, he made a long tour with his father. In his heart, he could not help wishing he were simply going to Vienna. But he enjoyed playing, now that he was allowed to play "real music." Everywhere his audiences loved hearing him. He had great talent and he was well prepared, thanks to his father and Herr Pfeiffer, and his other teachers.

As the time went by, Ludwig learned that the city of Bonn, his home, was a good place for a musician to be, even if it was not Vienna. The people of Bonn were music-loving people. There were singing societies and orchestras, and fine organs in the churches with master organists to play them. There was work, and appreciation, in Bonn for any musician.

Tobias Pfeiffer really believed in Ludwig's genius. He tried to find ways to help him. He arranged for Ludwig to hear more and more organ music, which he knew the boy loved.

Ludwig began to take lessons on the organ, and soon he was allowed to play for church services. One day, the court organist heard him at the church and offered to teach him.

In this teacher Ludwig found someone else who understood his longing to write music. Herr Neefe was delighted with Ludwig's compositions. "Very good, very good," he often said. "Yes, Ludwig, your music is exceedingly promising."

One day the organist asked him to compose something special. "Let me see what you can do with this march," Herr Neefe said. "Bring me some variations of its music next week. Or sooner, if you finish before then."

Ludwig went to work with a will and a happy enthusiasm. In three days, he had written nine pieces based on the music of the march. He took the nine variations to his teacher, and the master looked at them carefully.

To Ludwig's dismay, Herr Neefe shook his head solemnly.

"Ludwig, you did not make your variations according to the rules I know you have learned. You must do this again."

Ludwig scowled.

"Herr Neefe, must one always follow the old rules? I have made up new ones. I think the music is more beautiful this way—*my* way! Will you let me play it for you and show you?"

"My boy, you must write according to the rules while you are learning," the master said. "Even if the music does sound better another way. After all, who are you? When you become a great master of music yourself, then—and only then—will you have the right to put your own rules first."

"Yes, sir," said Ludwig, sadly. He had been so eager to show Herr Neefe his new ideas! He was even a little angry. But he rewrote the variations according to the rules, and his teacher was pleased.

"This is splendid, Ludwig. Now, I have a reward for you. From now on, you shall be my assistant organist. You have talent, my boy," Herr Neefe told him. "Better still, you work hard! Now, I shall send the music to be printed."

"What music, Herr Neefe?"

"These nine variations whose rules you frown upon."

"Herr Neefe!" shouted Ludwig. "I cannot wait!"

"It will be soon," Herr Neefe promised.

Sure enough, the music soon arrived. Ludwig's eyes sparkled as he read the words, "*Nine Variations on a March,* by Ludwig van Beethoven." It was a great honor for a twelve-year-old.

It was also a great honor to be assistant organist in Herr Neefe's church. Ludwig practiced hour after hour so that he would be ready to play whenever Herr Neefe needed him. He did so well that he was asked to play for rehearsals at the opera house and to conduct the orchestra. He was proud of his jobs, and proud to be earning money for his family.

Twelve-year-old Ludwig played for Eastern services in the great church when Herr Neefe had to be away.

"Look! A child is playing the organ!" someone in the congregation whispered. "Do you realize that is just a boy playing? Herr Neefe is not there!"

Soon everyone in the church realized that a young boy was taking Herr Neefe's place.

Ludwig could feel the warmth, excitement and

interest of the people. He was not nervous. He thought only of the music. He was wrapped in the beauty of the Easter music, and he played better than he had ever played before.

When the services were over, he put his scarf around his neck and started to run. Suddenly he bumped into Herr Neefe himself! The master had returned in time to hear part of Ludwig's playing.

"Maestro!" Ludwig said. "I—I hope you were not disappointed in me?"

"It could not have been more beautiful, Ludwig. No one could have done better. You are already a better pianist and organist than I! Indeed, as I listened I could not help feeling you are right about going to Vienna. I think the time has come. Let us hope you can go soon, and study with Mozart."

"Oh, Maestro, you know that is my dream. But you know also there is no hope. There is no money for me to make such a trip. I try to save what I am able to earn, but it is always needed. Somehow, I must find a way to earn the money. Oh, I must!"

Ludwig worked harder than ever. He did earn extra fees, but as before, the money was always needed at home. His mother was ill, and growing worse. Money had to be found for doctors and medicine, too. Sometimes Ludwig was sure he would never get to Vienna.

Five long years went by. The boy was nearly a young man, and still his great dream seemed far away. But he was a better musician and a harder worker than he had ever been.

Then one day, Herr Neefe, his face beaming with smiles, hurried to the Beethoven home with glorious news.

"Listen, everybody! The Elector has decided to provide the money for Ludwig to travel to Vienna. He has arranged for him to study with Mozart as well, at his expense!"

In a few days, young Beethoven stood in the home of Mozart. He looked awkward in his homespun clothes, his dark bushy hair was rumpled. He felt shy and embarrassed. But he was determined to do his best.

And he did. He played the pianoforte and he played it well.

But Mozart seemed disinterested, as if this was nothing unusual—just a prepared piece, played well enough. But still, it was something any number of young students might do.

Ludwig sensed how the great master felt. He thought very quickly. He must gain another chance before Mozart spoke. The master was about to dismiss him.

"Maestro, please!" said Ludwig. "Will you give

me a melody, a theme? Let me improvise for you."

For the first time since Ludwig had arrived, Mozart became interested. The boy was so excited! So intense! Asking for a melody — any melody — was what the Maestro liked. He went at once to the pianoforte, thought for a moment. Then he played a melody so difficult that no ordinary student could improve upon it.

The Maestro went to his music stand, preparing to work on his own manuscript as the boy played.

Ludwig van Beethoven was more excited than he had been in all his life. He was desperately hoping to please this man. Over and over he had said to himself, on the way to Vienna, "This is your chance. This is what you have dreamed of all your life."

Now he was frightened, and trying not to be. He must remember that he was a musician. He must remember all the people who had taught him and believed in him, beginning with his grandfather, long ago. Mozart was a master—the master he most admired. But the Beethovens were musicians, too!

Ludwig was pale, and he felt faint. But in his ears was the melody Mozart had just played for him. It was a beautiful melody, a theme he would love to improvise upon.

He touched the keys gently, silently fingering the scales. Suddenly, he took a deep breath and lifted his head high, closed his eyes and began to play. In his mind, in his heart, in his head, and on the pianoforte the melody Mozart had given him sang. It soared. It filled the air with beauty.

The Maestro turned from his manuscript, forgetting all about it. He looked in wonder at the youth and saw how lost he was in the music. Mozart sat down and listened with eyes closed. Again he looked at the boy, still playing, still lost in the music.

At just that moment, some friends arrived to visit Mozart. The Maestro, seeing them in the doorway, spoke. His words have gone down in the history of music:

"You hear! Then listen to me, my friends. Keep your eyes on this lad. He is going to make a noise in the world!"

Ludwig's black eyes burned with excitement and joy. Mozart was pleased with his music!

The days which followed were the happiest Ludwig could remember. He was in Vienna, and he was studying with the greatest maestro of all.

Beethoven's life was a hard one, often filled with disappointments and heartbreak. His mother died when he was eighteen, and the young man spent five more long years back in Bonn, working to support his family, before he returned to Vienna to live.

Deafness began in his late twenties, and finally he

was totally deaf. Then he could do no more performing and conducting. But though he could not hear it from the outside, he still heard music in his mind and heart. He composed more and more as his deafness increased.

He wrote: "I live only in my music, and no sooner is one thing done than another is begun. Often I must work on three or four things at once if I am to come near to the aim which I can feel. I will defy my fate of deafness insofar as possible, and when it makes me at times the most miserable of God's creatures, I will grapple with fate. It shall never drag me down."

It never did. Ludwig van Beethoven achieved fame for his music in his lifetime. He wrote by his own rules, as he had long wanted to do, and made the world take notice of his rules.

Today he is considered one of the great composers the world has had. The world is a better, more beautiful one because of the music Beethoven gave to it, and because of the strength, power and mighty spirit he showed in giving it.

FRANZ SCHUBERT

In the days when Vienna was the musical center of all Europe, a little boy was born who was to add to the glory of his birthplace. His name was Franz Schubert. The house where he was born . . . now a public inn, where visitors to Vienna often stay. There is a gray marble tablet over the door of the inn.

"FRANZ SCHUBERTS GEBURTSHAUS," it says—Franz Schubert's Birthplace. "31 January, 1797."

Franz Schubert was a very busy composer. He wrote more than six hundred songs; eight symphonies; operas, masses, chamber music, and many compositions for the piano. His work was known and admired in his lifetime. Yet he was always the most modest of composers.

He found it hard to believe that his work was great, though he loved it so much. He found it hard to believe that he deserved the honors that came to him. If he were able to visit his childhood home in

Vienna today, he would surely be surprised to see the marble tablet on the door, honoring his name.

Franz's father was a schoolteacher. He held his classes in that very house. Professor Schubert was the "Franz" in the family then, and the boy was "Franzel"—little Franz.

Professor Schubert often worried about how he could provide for all the needs of the family with his poor little salary. His wife, Elizabeth, was always cheerful and helpful. She reassured him.

"We shall manage, my dear," she always said. "Of course, we must be careful never to waste a single penny or a bit of precious food. So, please, try to stop worrying or you will not be able to teach. Then we shall be worse off than ever!"

Another day, she said, "Remember this, dear Franz. We have each other. And we have fine children. We are a happy family. That is enough to make up for many things we do not have."

Professor Schubert smiled. "Ah, Elizabeth, you are right. Franzel, you are looking very solemn. Do you not agree with Mama and Papa?"

The solemn little boy nodded his head firmly. "Yes, I do, Papa! I was thinking of all the good things we have. I think our pianoforte is the best of all. Is it not good that we can have it? Is it not a very great treasure, Mama?"

Frau Schubert smiled and nodded as she bent over her mending. "Yes, Franzel, we are indeed fortunate to have it, even though it is old and shabby. *Ach!* But when you play your little tunes on it, Franzel, it becomes something rare and beautiful. Play one of them now, dear, so Papa can hear. Go on!"

Little Franz began to smile. "Papa, would you like to hear what I played today to show Mama how music can say anything, even better than words?"

"*Ja*, Franzel! I should like very much to know how this is done. Then perhaps I could play music for my pupils instead of making speeches! Perhaps they would learn much faster."

"You are teasing, Papa?" asked Franz anxiously.

"Maybe, a little bit, but I am interested. Show me what you mean, and keep me waiting no longer!"

Franz ran to the pianoforte, climbed up on the shaky old stool and began to play. As he played, he explained his game.

"Papa," he asked, "what is this music saying? Can you tell?"

"Hm-m-m," said Professor Schubert as he thoughtfully stroked his chin. Then he clapped his hands. "I have it! It tells me there are soldiers marching."

"Yes, Papa, yes!" shouted Franz. "And this?" He played a gay little tune.

"That one is easy!" Professor Schubert laughed. "It is children dancing. No question about it."

"That is right, Papa! And this?"

"I know that one," Frau Schubert said quietly. "It is the vesper bells of our church. It sounds exactly as they do, each evening."

"You see, Papa! Music can say everything! Listen to it sing of sadness. Now, here is a storm! These are singing birds! This is moonlight. Isn't music a wonderful thing?"

"Very wonderful, Franzel. Your game is a delightful one. We shall play it in the schoolroom some day soon. Then all our pupils can enjoy it as we have. What do you think, Elizabeth?"

"That is a splendid idea," the mother said. "Also, I think our little Franzel has a very great talent. His music is not just a childish game, or an idle day-dream. It fills his life. I wish with all my heart he could have lessons with the best teachers in Vienna."

"Yes, you are right," said Professor Schubert. "The boy should have a chance to learn all he can of music. But lessons with good teachers would cost more money than we have to live on. However, I shall teach him what little I can on the violin. And perhaps his big brother Ignaz will help him learn proper technique for the pianoforte. Eh, Franzel! Shall we begin at once?"

So when Franz Schubert was seven years old, his music lessons were begun. To the amazement of his father and his older brother Ignaz, the little boy seemed to know as much as they did and could play far better. Professor Schubert was puzzled.

"My little son," he said, "you astonish me. I simply do not understand. Everything Ignaz and I try to tell you of music, you seem to know already. How have you learned so much about music without study?"

"I have studied by myself, Papa. I love music so much I had to learn. I could not help learning. People can teach themselves if they want to hard enough."

Franzel's family was very proud of him. Professor Schubert and Ignaz agreed that somehow they would find a way to earn some extra pennies, for better lessons than they themselves could give.

The boy's father spoke to Herr Holzer, choirmaster and organist at the family's church. And Herr Holzer promised to teach little Franz.

Franzel was overjoyed to study with a real musician. He had a lesson every day. Together he and Herr Holzer explored the wonders and beauties of the violin, the pianoforte and the organ. Herr Holzer also taught Franzel some of the things he would need to know to write music properly.

In less than four months, Choirmaster Holzer, in great excitement, went to see Professor Schubert.

"*Ach,* my friend! I have seen a miracle! Listen to me, Professor Schubert! Never have I seen the likes of that boy of yours. When I begin to teach him something new, he already knows it. 'How?' I ask. 'I don't know, sir,' he answers. 'I have always known that!'

"Then I give him problems in writing melody and harmony. I tell him to extemporize, to do it without taking time to think about it."

The musician waved his arms in amazement. "And you have never heard such music as he plays! It is correct! As well as beautiful! Sir, the truth is, he knows more about music than I do. He plays the instruments better than I do. He sings like an angel and he improvises like . . . like a master! He is so full of music he is brimming over with it!"

Herr Holzer stopped waving his arms around. He grew serious. "My friend, the child must go to the Choir School. He must be trained for the Imperial Chapel."

Professor Schubert looked at Franzel's teacher, who seemed so positive. He thought for a moment. Then, quietly he spoke:

"We must be very sure, Herr Holzer. Franzel is sensitive, so easily hurt. If he should try for such an honor — the Imperial Choir School! — before he is ready, he would fail. And that would break his heart. Or perhaps he is just not good enough. That, too, would break his heart. Do you think he could pass the tests, when so many boys fail?"

"I know he could!" Herr Holzer stamped around the room. "I know it! And he must begin now! No more time should be lost! It would be a pity and a crime to keep him back any longer."

"You seem very certain," said Professor Schubert. Sadly, he shook his head. "It is a great pity I have not the money for the school, and no way of raising it."

"Money, money, money!" said Herr Holzer in exasperation. "Money, is it? Well, I shall see that he takes the examinations under the Kapellmeister and the singing master. If he passes for them, he will not need any money! He will win a scholarship, if he passes! Did I say 'if'? Ridiculous! Franz Schubert cannot help but pass. Franz! Come here, at once!"

Franzel came running in. His teacher held him by his thin shoulders and announced, "You will prepare yourself at once, child, to take the examinations for the Choir School of Music."

Franzel could hardly believe it. The Choir School was what he wanted most in the world. Music,

music, all day long. But the examinations were said to be very, very hard to pass. Could he possibly pass them? Could he really do it?

"I have to do it." Franzel spoke aloud, though he was talking to himself. "I must not be afraid. I must work very hard."

Herr Holzer solemnly agreed. "No, you must not be afraid. And yes, you must work very hard."

Franz Schubert did work very hard. On an October day in 1808, when Franz was eleven years old, the examinations were held. There were many other boys, most of them well dressed. They were very different in manner and background from Franz. Some of them whispered and nudged each other when they saw the small shy boy. Franz was dressed in an old suit, worn and mended, but very clean.

It was no easy thing for Franz to stand in that chapel before masters and boys he had never seen before, ready to answer the many questions which would be put to him. He felt like running away.

He was afraid. But he knew that he had studied very hard for this chance. And he knew it was the only chance he would ever have to learn everything there was to learn about music.

"I must not spoil it," he thought. "Without music I could not live. If I should fail, I will fail Papa and Mama and Ignaz and Herr Holzer, too. This I cannot do. Franz Schubert, pay attention," he told himself. "Pass this examination."

Then the questions began. At the first question, Franz answered in such a low voice that the Kapellmeister spoke rather sharply.

"You must speak up in a clear, distinct voice!" he said.

The other boys snickered. The singing master rapped for silence and Franz answered the question again, clearly, firmly and correctly. After that he spoke well, without hesitation, during the entire session.

After the oral examination, each child played an instrument, sang a song and improvised. When it was Franz's turn, he stepped forward eagerly. This was his joy! This he loved more than anything. Had not Herr Holzer told him he could sing like an angel and improvise better than he himself was able to do? It was fun! He loved it, and he did it often at home for a game.

For the examiners, Franz played not one instrument, but three—the violin, the pianoforte and the organ. Then he began to improvise on themes given to him by the Kapellmeister. Soon the other boys quieted down and listened happily. Franz was then asked to play and sing some of his own compositions. Then, to sing the songs of the Choir.

Suddenly the singing master jumped up and ran to the astonished boy. He embraced him, kissed him on both cheeks and shouted "Bravo! Bravo!"

"Franz Schubert, that was beautiful! Beautiful! Put on the uniform of the Imperial Chorister, child, and honor it. You play the music like an angel. You sing it like an angel and you compose it like an angel. Ach! You *are* an angel! How grateful we are that you have come to us!"

The Kapellmeister nodded in agreement. The new boys as well as those already in the Choir School applauded. Franz was overwhelmed.

"You mean, Sir, I have passed the examination?" he asked wonderingly.

"Most certainly you have passed the examination, Franz Schubert, and with the highest honors since I came here many years ago."

The singing master realized how modest and earnest this boy was, how much this meant to him. He nodded understandingly as Franz almost whispered, "Then, sir, I shall be able to study music here, all day? Every day?"

"Yes, child," said the singing master.

"And shall I be able to learn the music of the masters? Beethoven, Bach, Mozart, Haydn?"

"Indeed yes, my boy. This is required."

Then Franz began to believe his good fortune.

"In all my dreams I did not think this could happen. Thank you, Maestro, with all my heart!"

The Kapellmeister and the singing master smiled at each other over the boy's head. All their boys enjoyed being there, but never had they seen such joy as that of young Franz Schubert.

Working and learning at the great school, Franz lived in a world of dreams come true, and he was grateful for every moment of it. One of his greatest joys was composing music. Every scrap of paper he could find, he filled with melodies that sang in his heart.

Herr Spaun, leader of the school orchestra, noticed Franz the first day he came. Listening to the opening music, he turned to see who was playing so cleverly. That evening he described the child to the singing master.

"There is an exceptional new boy," he said. "A small, bushy-haired child with spectacles."

"Ah, yes," answered the master with a smile. "I am not surprised that you noticed. His name is Franz Schubert."

Herr Spaun was a rather distant, severe looking man. Franz admired him tremendously and longed to talk with him, but he was afraid to do so. Then one day Herr Spaun spoke to Franz.

"Wait a moment, Franz. Sit here, beside me."

"Yes, sir," answered Franz breathlessly. He wondered if something could be wrong with his work.

"I have been watching you," said Herr Spaun. "You have a great and rare talent, my boy. And I am told you compose music as well as you play it."

"Yes, sir. I mean—" Franz began to stammer. "I mean I do compose, sir, but I do not know how well. I love to write music. I hear it all around, everywhere. So much of it, I'd write lots more if I could afford to buy more paper."

Franz stopped, embarrassed at what he had said.

But Herr Spaun threw back his head, slapped his forehead with his hand and shouted, "Listen to the boy! If he could afford to buy more paper he would write more music! Well, Franz Schubert—you shall have all the music paper you want, from now on! Why? How? Because I will give it to you. All you want, every morning. Just come to my desk. It will be an honor to give you the paper."

Sundays and holidays Franz spent at home, where he and his family made music together. Herr Schubert played the 'cello. Brothers Ferdinand and Ignaz played the first and second violins, and Franz the viola. Often the music they played was composed by Franz.

Sometimes Herr Schubert would make a mistake. Franz paid no attention unless the mistake was repeated. Then he would say, shyly and gently, "Herr father, something must be wrong there."

Those were the happiest years of Franz Schubert's life—those years of music in school with his beloved masters, and music at home with his beloved family.

When Franz was seventeen, another honor came to him. His first large piece of church music was played in Herr Holzer's church. It was a proud day for the Schuberts. Franz conducted, Ferdinand Schubert played the organ, and Herr Holzer led the choir in the first performance of Franz' *Mass in F*.

In the audience was a famous music master of Vienna. He praised Franz warmly, and offered to teach him. This was a great honor, too, for the famous teachers were always busy. Franz studied with the master for many months. He knew there was always something more a musician must learn!

It is astonishing to discover that Franz Schubert composed such a great quantity of art songs, or *Lieder*. These songs require singers who are capable of understanding, to the fullest extent, the meaning of the poems which are set to music.

Franz was not always so free to work and study as he was in the happy school years. But whenever he was playing or composing, he was happy, no matter what happened. There were bitter, hard times in later years. But in spite of them, Franz's life was always fine and beautiful. He made it so with his goodness, his gentle spirit, and his love for the music he could hear in everything, everywhere.

FREDERIC CHOPIN

The very night he was born, little Frederic Chopin heard music. Peasants from the neighborhood played a gay, happy serenade outside the window of Madame Chopin's room. They had brought their fiddles and horns, their singers and flutes, and the starry night air tingled with the gaiety of Polish songs and dances. It was February, 1810, in the village of Zelazowa-Wola, about thirty miles from Warsaw.

Justine and Nicolas Chopin were happily married. Nicolas was French by birth and education; Justine was a beautiful Polish girl he had met when he came to work in Poland. The family atmosphere combined French and Polish language and customs.

At the time of Frederic's birth, his family lived a busy, stimulating life on a great country estate. There Nicolas tutored the children of a noble family. So Frederic Chopin was one of the few great composers who enjoyed a happy childhood with a comfortable home and loving parents. He also had two adoring older sisters.

One day soon after the baby boy learned to crawl, Louise, the second sister, ran to her mother. "Mama, come quickly! Something must be wrong with Frederic. Yesterday and today, he crawls only as far as the piano. Then he sits there, not making a sound! He won't move."

Madame Chopin picked up her skirts and ran. Frederic smiled when he saw his mother coming. Then he leaned as close to the piano strings as he could get, and listened intently.

"Frederic, are you all right?" asked Madame Chopin, the way mothers always talk to babies, as if they could answer back. This time, Frederic did. He nodded his head and pointed to the strings.

When Madame Chopin went closer, the baby clapped his hands and laughed. For a moment, she looked puzzled. Then she walked over to the piano with firm steps. Frederic laughed again and pointed to the strings.

Then Madame Chopin picked up the baby, swung him in her arms, and laughingly kissed him.

"Frederic!" she said. "It is the vibration of the strings you like to hear! Don't you see, Louise? Whenever anyone walks or moves heavily, the strings vibrate. Frederic has discovered this and that is why he won't move away from the piano. I am sure now that he has great love for music."

"Oh, Mama, he is just a baby. How do you know?" Louise looked very puzzled.

"Well, the first time I played for him, he began to cry. I was afraid he did not like music. Then I found out he was crying because I had stopped playing!"

"But how could you know that?" asked Louise.

"Because, darling, he pulled my skirts and pointed to the harpsichord. So I played again, and he began to smile. I always take him with me to the piano now."

Louise laughed. "He's a funny baby." Then she ran to call her older sister. "Isabelle! Isabelle! The mystery is solved! It is to hear the vibrations of the strings that Fritz won't budge from under the piano."

When Frederic was about eight months old, his father was appointed supervisor and professor of French at a French school in Warsaw. Although the appointment was a great honor, the family regretted moving from the country to the city.

Soon after the move, another little girl, who looked exactly like Frederic, was born. Her name was Emilie, and she was Frederic's constant companion.

A few years later, when Frederic was about five years old, the children gave a play to honor their father's birthday. Written by Frederic and Emilie, it was gay and funny. Everyone had a fine time.

That night, long after the house was quiet, the children's nurse thought she heard a noise. Quickly lighting her candle, she saw at once that Frederic had disappeared! Smothering a cry, she hurried out of the room just in time to see him running down the stairs in his nightgown.

"Good Heavens," she thought to herself. "He's walking in his sleep. I must be careful not to frighten the child."

Quietly, she followed the little boy down the stairs and into the parlor. To her astonishment, Frederic climbed up to the bench in front of his mother's piano. He fingered the keys for a moment until he found a melody he had often heard his mother play. Then he played it himself.

"Glory be!" thought the nurse. "The child is playing the music in his sleep! Or else he is quite completely bewitched! I must run and tell Madame Chopin and the Master, and if need be, the doctor himself."

But when the Chopins saw what was going on, they motioned for Nurse to be quiet. Soon, the three little girls, the cook, and everybody else in the house crowded into the doorway of the little parlor to listen to the music. Frederic was playing all the songs and waltzes, mazurkas and folk music he had heard his mother play.

Suddenly Madame Chopin realized the room was far too cold for the little boy to be sitting there so long in his night clothes.

She tiptoed over to Frederic, speaking very gently as she did so. "It sounded so lovely, we all came down to listen, Fritz dear. But it is very cold here, and you are dressed far too lightly. Nurse will fix a little hot goat's milk to keep us from catching cold. Then, off to bed we shall go, all of us!"

"Mama! I'm sorry!" said Frederic.

"Why should you be sorry?" said his mother. "You have done nothing wrong, only something very nice. I had no idea you could play like that!"

"Neither did I," said Louise, excitedly. "Now we can have music in our next play! How can you play without any lessons or practice, Fritz? You play those waltzes better than I do, and I've been working on them for weeks."

"Me too," said Isabella. "Imagine!"

"Shh! No more conversation, my dears. Just run on to bed. Off to bed, everyone!"

When the house was quiet again, Madame Chopin smiled in the darkness. She said softly, "Louise said little Fritz played better than she! My dear, he plays better than I, and though, of course, I am an amateur, I am not considered too bad."

"You play beautifully, with great tenderness and expression," answered her husband.

"Not with the touch of Frederic," said Madame Chopin thoughtfully. "It reminds me of stories I have heard about Mozart as a child. I believe we have a musical genius in our little boy. Remember how he used to crawl under the piano to listen to the strings vibrate? And how he cried when I stopped playing? We must arrange for lessons at once. Talent should be encouraged."

The very next day, Adalbert Zywny, the best-known music master in Warsaw, came to see Professor Chopin.

"This is luck!" said Frederic's father. "I was just going to call on you."

Then he told Professor Zywny about Frederic's unusual interest in and aptitude for music.

"The boy should certainly be encouraged," said Professor Zywny. "May I hear him play?"

"Remember," said Frederic's father, "he has never had a lesson. Until last night, none of us had heard him play."

"I shall take that into consideration," said Professor Zywny.

They were just in time to hear Madame Chopin finishing a waltz, and Frederic asking to try it. The two men stood with the boy's mother, listening. A smile on Professor Zywny's face grew bigger as Frederic played.

"Do you think—" began Madame Chopin when Frederic had finished the waltz.

"I think this boy is a musician," said the Professor. "Frederic, you seem to have an instinct for the piano. Something tells me you could play music on it we have never heard—music that is turning over and over in your head."

Frederic looked at the master as though he had performed a trick of magic. "Why, how did you know that, sir?"

"Oh, we musicians have a language all our own," Professor Zywny said. "Suppose you play for us now. Play that tune I think you are hearing in your head."

Frederic began to play a variation of the waltz his mother had been playing. As he did so, he held his head as she always did. Then he imitated Isabelle and Louise at the piano. Finally, playing a melody with deep bass tones, he mimicked his father and Professor Zywny, too.

Professor Zywny was delighted.

"Good! Very good, indeed. I am glad you can have fun with your music, Frederic. That means you, yourself, enjoy it, so all who hear it will enjoy it with you.

To Frederic's father, he said, "It will be an honor, a privilege, and a very great pleasure to have Frederic come to me for lessons. The lessons will help him to understand the technique, the theory of this music for which he has such great natural talent."

It was not long before Professor Zywny had taught Frederic how to write the music he composed. So the boy and Emilie were able to write and perform a play with music for their father's next birthday.

Soon Frederic had the opportunity to test his musicianship before a larger audience. Professor Zywny arranged for a large private concert in the winter before Frederic was eight years old. It was a great success. He was proclaimed a second Mozart!

A few days after the concert, a very pompous cavalry officer, wearing much gold braid and riding a magnificent black horse, stopped in front of the Chopin house. His uniform showed that he was in the service of the Grand Duke Constantine, brother of the Tsar and Governor of Warsaw. He sent a page to the door with a message for Madame Chopin. The excited children gathered around her.

"What is it, Mama?" asked Frederic. "Who sent it?"

"Oh, Mama, is he not from the palace?" asked Isabelle.

"The palace!" echoed Louise and Emilie. "What did he want? What happened?"

"Goodness, children," said Madame Chopin laughingly. "Give us a chance to find out. If it is good news, I shall read it to you at once. If not, you shan't hear a word. . . . Now, don't look so crestfallen. I am only teasing. Of course it is good news . . . well, not bad, in any case. Listen: 'His Imperial Highness requests the pleasure of young Frederic Chopin's presence at 4:00 P. M. in the salon of the Princess Lowicka.' "

"Four o'clock!" said Frederic, astonished. "Does that mean today? It's already past one o'clock!"

"Apparently so," answered his mother, as the girls jumped up and down squealing in their excitement.

"However, can he be ready in time?" asked Louise. Little Emilie put her nose in the air and strutted around Frederic with the air of a princess.

Everyone was laughing and talking at once when Professor Chopin came to see what had happened. "Someone said one of the Governor's cavalry officers was here. Is anything wrong?"

Madame Chopin handed the note to her husband. He looked at it, then at the family.

"Hmmm," he said thoughtfully. "Suppose we all sit down for a moment. You realize, of course, that notes like this are in the nature of a command. Frederic is undoubtedly being commanded to repeat his concert for the benefit of the Princess Lowicka and her friends. She is a very charming person, Frederic. She will be most gracious and correct. It will be easy to conduct yourself as you have been taught, in her presence.

"However, the Grand Duke may give you a bit of a shock. At times he is overbearing, ridiculously pompous, and often downright rude. You must be sure to keep this in mind and ignore it completely. Of course, I need not remind you that you are a gentleman. Remember, too, while you play, to forget everything but your music. You cannot help but play well."

"Yes, Frederic," said Madame Chopin with a loving smile, "Papa is quite right. You have already practiced more than enough for one day, so you need not worry about that. Suppose, now, you go and bathe while the girls and I prepare your court costume."

"Court costume!" said Frederic, stopping on the way to the door. "I have no court costume. Do I need one?"

"Of course not, darling," said Madame Chopin

gaily, searching through her mending basket. "It will be your court costume from now on, if you wear it to court today! The costume you wore for the concert is the one I mean. I think I saw a tiny rip on the lace of the collar. Fetch it for me, girls, and we shall see that it is ripless and spotless by the time Frederic finishes his bath."

So that afternoon, little eight-year-old Frederic Chopin presented himself at the palace promptly at four. He was conducted at once to the salon of the Princess Lowicka. When he arrived in his 'court costume,' the velvet coat with the English collar, he was very much admired.

But the Grand Duke, elegant in his polished boots and magnificent uniform, merely smirked like a comic character in a play. Pretending not to notice the Grand Duke's rather insulting manner, Frederic was most polite as he had promised his parents he would be. The Grand Duke then bowed with an exaggerated flourish, clicked his heels and seemed very amused. He spoke in affected French, thinking Frederick would not understand.

"Ah, *oui, oui, oui, vous-êtes Monsieur* Chopin, eh? You are *Monsieur Chopin?* Hmmmm. *Monsieur* Chopin!"

Three times "Monsieur Chopin" bowed in answer to the Grand Duke. Then he answered courteously in good French — better French than the Duke's.

The Grand Duke could say nothing more but, "Very well, *sir*, play something for us, at once."

"Thank you, your Excellency," said little Frederic, with another courtly bow. Then he bowed toward the Princess Lowicka, who was watching with an admiring smile. "It is that for which I have come. It gives me great pleasure to play for the charming lady. Your Highness," said Frederic with another bow.

Then he sat down before the piano. As he ran his delicate fingers over the keys, he smiled with delight. It was in perfect tune, a beautiful sounding instrument. Frederic played a few of his own compositions. They were applauded enthusiastically, but the Grand Duke looked a little bored.

Frederic smiled to himself, bowed toward the arrogant gentleman, and began to improvise in march time. The result was a stirring military march. The Grand Duke was a true soldier, and he began to keep time with his cane, forgetting this was a dignified tea concert.

When Frederic finished, he bowed again in the direction of the Grand Duke, and that gentleman was completely won over by the child. He commanded the director of the Guard's Band to listen, notebook in hand, while Frederic repeated the martial music. Thn he saw to it that the music was copied and given to all members of the band.

Shortly after this, little Frederic Chopin had the very great thrill of seeing the soldiers march to his own music. In fact, Frederic's first concert was the beginning of a series of musical triumphs for the little boy. He loved every minute of every one of them.

After a few lessons, he was often asked to play the organ during Mass in the Chapel of The Visitation. One time, when he forgot himself and began to improvise, the musicians and singers were so interested in Frederic's music they forgot to sing and play their own parts. They were quite abruptly brought back to reality when the director appeared at the top of the organ loft.

"Hsst! Gentlemen! Ladies! *What* is happening?" he asked.

Everywhere Frederic was applauded. Although he was excited and grateful, he was never spoiled by all the admiration he received. His gentle, careful training had developed an unusual child prodigy.

During this exciting period in his boyhood, Chopin felt a tremendous love for his native country, Poland. And the country inspired his music. He found music in the countryside, the shepherd's flute, the peasant dances, the city's official ceremonies. He and Emilie portrayed all these things in the music plays they gave for their parents.

One day, Professor Zywny called in Frederic's parents for a mysterious conference. He said that he had nothing more to teach the brilliant boy. "I wish him to continue his training under Joseph Elsner, the greatest teacher of music theory, counterpoint, and advanced construction in Warsaw." And so arrangements were made for Frederic to have a new teacher.

One day, Professor Chopin went into the parlor to watch Frederic practice a very difficult piece of music. Professor Chopin was always careful not to interfere with his children's activities. But when he saw Frederic's hands that afternoon, he spoke without thinking.

"Frederic Chopin! Your hands! What have you done?"

Frederic laughed. "Don't look so worried, Papa," he said. "I am composing, and I want some chords I cannot reach. So I'm using this stretcher. I invented it myself."

The small wooden "stretcher," as he called it, kept his fingers farther apart than he could stretch them without it.

"But, Frederic," said his father anxiously, "I think that other pianists have tried that, too. They could do great harm to their fingers — permanent harm."

"I know, Papa. But that is because they forced it. This invention of mine just helps me to keep my fingers farther apart. It doesn't hurt a bit."

Then Frederic showed his father how he was unable to reach a chord without the stretcher. With it, he could easily reach.

"Soon I will be able to stretch my fingers far enough without it," he said.

"Suppose we make a bargain," his father said. "If the doctor says it is harmless after he examines it, you may continue to use it. Is that fair?"

"Yes, Papa," Frederic said gratefully. "You and Mama are always more than fair."

Frederic suddenly felt very happy about his family. He realized how much his parents had helped him study the music that he loved, and how unselfish his sisters had been.

It was just at this happy time that misfortune and tragedy struck the family. Emilie, the sister so much like Frederic, fell ill with a lung ailment which both children had suffered many times before. This time, Emilie did not recover.

When Frederick became ill soon after Emilie's death, the Chopin household was changed and sorrowful, indeed. Frederic's parents had almost lost hope. Then help came from a friend, Prince Radziwill. Frederic was invited to go and live in the prince's country palace for as long as he liked.

At the palace, many noble boys his own age were training for the cavalry and army life. But they studied the same lessons as Frederic. So, he could continue his education, and devote time to music.

"Now what do you think of this invitation, my dear?" said Professor Chopin to his wife.

"I think it will save our Frederic's life, if it is not too late." Frederic's mother had tears in her eyes. "Let us hope and pray it will not be."

To the great joy and gratitude of the Chopin family, the invitation had not come too late. Frederic soon grew well enough to leave his bed. So he went to live in the country palace of a great Polish family—the kind of life he had been born into.

Prince Radziwill was a musician himself, and he thought Frederic a true genius. The prince encouraged the boy to give many concerts at the court and to spend all the time he wished on music.

The country estate was a wonderful place for a boy who loved both music and the outdoors. Even though he missed his family, Frederic began to regain his health and gay spirits. There were many young companions his age. He enjoyed their exciting court life and began to compose some wonderful dance music for the court balls.

The young sons of Polish noblemen whom Frederic met at the palace were far more interested in hunting and cavalry training than in music. Sometimes they teased Frederic about his lack of interest in sports and his great devotion to music. Whenever this happened, Frederic would say something like this:

"I must confess I am stupid and poor at all outdoor sports, except walking. You ought to see me on a horse! I look like a monkey riding on a bear in a circus. And shooting! There, I am even worse. But aren't we all made differently? I admire you accomplished athletes, for your skill in hunting and soldiering, and I hope you admire whatever skill I may have in music."

Then Frederic would act out in music and gestures what he had said. There would be a crashing, galloping tempo for the soldiers, and gentle, timid passages for himself. The young men would roar with laughter, and feel a great respect for Frederic.

Everyone in Prince Radziwill's court was fond of him. He always showed respect for his elders and had time to play with the children, give them lessons, or entertain them.

While he was living at the palace, two of his compositions were published. The sight of his own music, actually printed for others to use, was the most exciting thing Frederic had ever known, in all his fifteen years.

He studied and practiced and spent even more time composing, after that. It was good that he was able to live in the country; for when he finished his schooling, he was well and strong again.

The time had come for Frederic Chopin to take his rightful place in the world of music. Two years of constant study and practice had made him into an artist. And his own compositions must have a larger hearing, too, his friends and teachers said.

Professor Elsner made arrangements for a concert tour for Frederic. It would begin in Vienna, and reach all the important cities of Europe. There was to be a farewell concert in Warsaw, as well.

What a farewell concert it was! All the Chopin family and friends, the stable-boys and the music-loving peasants from the chateau; the students, the professors, the nobility, the royal family, crowded into the concert hall. Best of all for young Frederic, Constantia Gladowska, his favorite singer, was the soloist. And Frederic Chopin himself was called back for bow after bow.

Then the concert was followed by a dinner given by Professor Elsner and Professor Zywny for Frederic's family and closest friends. All of them accompanied Frederic to the outskirts of the city, following the stagecoach in carriages. There, Professor Elsner presented Frederic with a small silver bowl, engraved with his name and filled with Polish soil.

Frederic looked very young indeed as he brushed the tears from his eyes, and made his farewell to his family, teachers, and friends.

"I shall devote my life and my work," he said, "to bring honors to the glory of Poland and to you, its wonderful people."

That was the goal seventeen-year-old Frederic Chopin set for himself when he left Poland. He never returned.

While Frederic was in Vienna, he heard of the siege of Warsaw. First he put his thoughts into music, the tragic and beautiful study, "Etude in C Minor." Then he wrote to tell his father he wanted to come home to fight for Poland.

Impatiently, he waited for the letter that would tell him how the journey could be arranged. When a letter from his father finally arrived, Frederic tore it open eagerly and read:

"My dear Frederic: All of us read your letter with deep interest and gratitude. Your teachers then showed it to the head of one of our regiments. The answer from them as well as from those of us at home is this: 'There is no way in this world in which you can help your beloved Poland and its people better than to glorify them with your music.' Indeed, because of your recurrent lung illnesses you could not even be accepted as a soldier, so you need have no fear that there is any misunderstanding about your patriotism. It is well understood by all."

Frederic Chopin renewed the vow he had made the night he left Warsaw. In the following years, he never failed to give his life and his work to make it come true—in spite of ill health, poverty, or misfortune. There were many moments of glory which made the hard times easier to bear.

Prince Radziwill introduced the young musician to the world of art and music in Paris. His concerts were loved, his compositions played and admired by the finest artists of his day.

When the great Robert Schumann heard him play, he said, "Hats off, gentlemen, a genius!"

Franz Liszt called Chopin the "soul of the piano" and publicly declared that no composer had ever written such sublime music for that instrument.

So Frederic Chopin fulfilled his promise to Poland.

The little bowl of Polish soil was with him when he died in Paris. At his funeral, Constantia Gladowska sang the aria she had sung for his farewell concert in Warsaw, when he was seventeen.

All of us who hear his music are richly rewarded by the dedication of Frederic Chopin.

GIUSEPPE VERDI

Once upon a time, in the little mountain village of Roncole, near Busseto, Italy, Carlo Verdi and his wife Luigia kept a small inn and supply shop for the mountain workers. They were a devoted, hard-working young couple and were completely happy when their son was born on October 10, 1813.

Because Giuseppe was his patron saint, the baby was christened Giuseppe Verdi. From the beginning, the healthy, happy little boy seemed to love the sound of music. Luigia was delighted, for she loved to sing. Every evening, the baby fell asleep to the soft tones of a lullaby.

One evening as she sang to the baby, Luigia looked up and saw Carlo standing in the doorway. He was standing straight, tensely alert, as if straining to hear some far-off sound. Luigia sat frozen with terror. She had never seen her husband look like that.

There had been talk that day about a battle, and

a rumor that German and Russian soldiers were marching through the Italian countryside, plundering as they went. But surely there could be no danger here in this peaceful spot. Even now, the bells in the tower of the tiny cathedral were sounding gently.

Carlo gave a sudden start, then motioned for Luigia to be silent. Quickly he crouched beside her and whispered urgently. "Luigia, I hear them! Listen carefully, you must not allow the baby to make a sound. Cover his mouth with your kerchief if he wakens. Run to the church as quickly as you can run! Climb up the stairway to the tower and hide."

"But, Carlo, you must come with me!"

"I'll be all right here. I'll give them anything they ask for to be rid of them quickly. Hurry, Luigia! Wait there until everything is quiet in the village. I'll come for you when they have gone. Hurry!"

Quickly they embraced; silently Luigia ran, covering little Giuseppe with her shawl. Carlo began to carry pieces of firewood into the tavern, whistling merrily as if he had not a care in the world.

Soon the soldiers came shouting and bragging of their victories. Everywhere they demanded food and wine as they passed through the town. They helped themselves to whatever they could find at the inn. When it was dark, they started out again, marching past the square. Some went into the church.

High in the tower sat Luigia. She rocked Giuseppe in her arms, whispering words of comfort. Softly she sang over and over:

"Sleep my darling, peace attend thee,
Safe in my arms, sleep, baby, sleep . . ."

The moon was high in the blue-gray sky before the village was quiet again. Someone moaned, a child cried heartbrokenly not far away. From her hiding place, Luigia could hear the sounds. Her throat was so tight she could not make a sound, herself. Her own baby began to stir restlessly in her arms. Then she heard her name.

"Luigia! Can you hear me? Are you all right? Are you there, Luigia? And the baby? It is all right now. They have gone!"

With a great sob of relief, Luigia climbed down the dark stair to meet her husband.

After that night in the church tower, Luigia noticed that whenever Giuseppe heard music he was happy. Even so, she was unprepared for what happened one morning several years later. Giuseppe's eyes had a dreamy, far-away look in them, and he had no appetite. Carlo and Luigia thought he was ill.

"Tell me, Giuseppe, what is the matter? Does something hurt?" his mother asked.

"It was called a spinet," said Giuseppe dreamily.

"What is the child talking about?" Luigia asked her husband.

"Spinet, Mama," Giuseppe said, his eyes shining. "Spinet. Papa, could we have one?"

"Goodness, child," said Luigia, with a laugh. "Only rich people can afford a spinet. Where did you see one?"

Giuseppe made the longest speech in his four years. "At the house of Maestro Baistrocchi, the church organist. When he saw me, he said Signora Baistrocchi had some fresh cakes and please to come in for some. So I went in and saw it. The Maestro said it was a spinet, that I could play it if I wanted to. He clapped, too, and he said I could come and play on it whenever I wanted to. But if we had one at home, I could play on it all the time!"

After the little boy ran out to play, Luigia asked, "What can we do, Carlo? Is there any way that we could save enough to buy a spinet? Perhaps an old one?"

"I wish we could," answered Carlo. "I wish we could. The child sings like an angel."

"Yes, and he runs to the church every time he hears Signor Baistrocchi practicing or playing for choir rehearsals. It is very nice of the Maestro to let Giuseppe play on his spinet. . . ."

Luigia went over to the fireplace and took down

the little box where she put a penny every time she could spare one. She shook gently, then made a sad little face and shrugged her shoulders. "No, it would take forever that way."

Carlo smiled. "Not if we both put in a penny whenever we possibly can! And sometimes when we think we cannot! We shall call it Giuseppe's Spinet Box, and here is the first penny!"

"Mama, Papa! Oh just think of it!" Giueseppe ran in breathless with excitement. "Think of it! I heard that a fine organist is going to play for vespers in Busseto this afternoon.

"Are you not going today, Papa? You said you had to get more coffee and sugar for the inn. Let me go with you, Papa. Please!"

"Oh no!" said Luigia. "No, Giuseppe. What are you thinking of? It is three miles to Busseto. Imagine a four-year-old boy walking three miles, six miles altogether. And Papa cannot carry you. No!"

"Please, Mama, please," Giuseppe begged earnestly. "I can walk that far. Please let me go."

"What do you think, Carlo?" asked Luigia.

Carlo Verdi nodded slowly, as he prepared his baskets, fastened his heavy sandals and reached for his cap. "My dear ones, I think we should at least try. If Giuseppe does not get too tired, we shall know it is a good idea. If Giuseppe must give up before we reach Busseto, we know it is not a good idea. How else can we tell?"

"Thank you, Papa and Mama! We're going! We're going to hear the music in Busseto!"

Giuseppe was so happy and excited Luigia could not help laughing as she waved good-by.

As the boy and father drew near the town of Busseto, Giuseppe almost trembled with excitement. He put his hand in his father's and looked up at him with a smile. Carlo Verdi smiled back, patted the boy on the shoulder and knelt down to smooth his hair and straighten his jacket as Luigia always did before entering the church.

"Yes, we are almost there, my son. You have walked like a young soldier. You must like the music very very much indeed to be willing to walk so far to hear it."

"I do, Papa," answered Giuseppe solemnly. "More than anything! Except you and Mama, of course."

"Ah, that is good to hear!" Carlo Verdi laughed. "Now, when we reach the church you go inside while I do the buying in the market. By the time vespers are over, I shall be through, and I shall come for you."

"Yes, Papa. Listen! The music is just beginning!"

Giuseppe began to run and Carlo followed him

quickly. "Don't forget, Giuseppe. Be sure to wait for me."

"Yes, Papa, yes!" And Giuseppe hastily hugged his father and ran into the church. There he sat and listened quietly to the beautiful organ music, silently humming the melodies to himself. He smiled with pleasure as he thought, "How good this makes me feel! How happy! Every day Papa comes to the market in Busseto, I shall come."

It seemed not more than minutes before the great organ was silent, the church almost empty. Giuseppe walked out as if in a dream, just in time to be lifted up in his father's arms.

"You did not even see me," teased Carlo. "I have been listening, too, for some time! It was very beautiful."

"And I am going again, every time you come to Busseto, Papa. I shall hear Maestro Baistrocchi all the other days in Roncole. And some day I shall be a musician, and I shall play beautiful music, too."

Papa Verdi laughed delightedly at his earnest little boy and swung him up high in the air. "Come, Mama will have supper ready. You may ride on my shoulders if you like," he offered, even though he had heavy baskets to carry.

"No, Papa, I like to walk. May I come to Busseto with you each week? May I, Papa?"

"Yes, Giuseppe," answered Carlo soberly. "I truly believe you walk faster than I do. Yes, you may come and listen to your beloved music."

And that is what happened. Every week for three years, Giuseppe went with his father to Busseto to listen to the music. Every day, he listened to the organist in the church of Roncole. And every day, he went to visit another good friend—the parish priest, who owned an old spinet. Whenever the busy priest had time, he helped Giuseppe learn the names of the notes he struck—the scales.

One day just before supper, Giuseppe joined his father in the shop. "Papa, I want to ask you something. The priest is very busy with sick people, weddings and things, and I almost never get to play his spinet any more. When Mozart was my age, he played concerts and composed music. He played the harpsichord and the violin and the organ and everything."

"Well, I don't know too much about music," Carlo Verdi answered, "or about Mozart. They say he played for the Pope and that he was a genius."

"Papa, I know that not all musicians can be geniuses. But they must have a chance to play music! The priest has an old spinet. He has no time to play it. Maybe we could buy it! It is old, but it sounds nice. What do you think, Papa?"

"Hmmm." Carlo Verdi smiled. "Well, I think, Giuseppe, that it is almost time for supper, and that it should be rather special tonight. Or have you forgotten that today is October the tenth in the year of 1820?"

"No, Papa, I have not forgotten," answered Giuseppe trying to smile.

"But you seem to have forgotten what that day means to this family!"

"No. Papa. It is my birthday. I am seven years old. I know that Mama has made special cookies and my favorite pasta. But all I can think about is how much I want to be able to play music, to learn enough to compose it, to be able to play the organ some time. I am much too old not to know more about music!"

Giuseppe looked so dejected that his mother ran to him with a worried look, as she came to call them in.

"What is it my son? Are you ill?"

"No Mama. Thank you. I am all right. I wish I could earn some money."

"Giuseppe is unhappy because he can live no longer without a spinet, he thinks," said Carlo. "He must learn we cannot always have everything we want in this world."

Just then, the parish priest came in with a gift for Giuseppe, wrapped in coarse brown paper.

"Am I too early?" he asked, looking anxiously at the little boy and his parents. You are busy. I shall return later." He started to go, but Luigia stopped him.

"Don't go, Father. You are just in time to show Giuseppe his birthday surprise. After that, you will join us for supper."

"Thank you," said the gentle priest. "You are very kind. It will be a pleasure for me to share this happy occasion."

"Ah, that makes our celebration a most festive one," said Carlo Verdi. "Now, let us first go to the parlor and see the birthday surprise. Father, you will enter first, if you please, and next, our birthday boy, Giuseppe . . . ."

Giuseppe looked and cried out, "Papa! Mama! Father! A spinet! A real spinet, right in our own parlor! A spinet that I can play every day!"

But the spinet was too wonderful. Giuseppe could not say another word. He sat down as if spellbound, then he fingered the keys. Before the astonished little group, he played a tender plaintive melody, very simple and very beautiful.

When he had finished playing the melody, Giuseppe forgetting the others in his deep interest, began to strike chords, one after another. Suddenly the quiet was broken by a loud clapping of hands at the open window, followed by a jolly shout of "Bravo!"

Realizing that he was not alone, Giuseppe looked up, surprised and embarrassed.

"Come, come, Giuseppe," said the voice at the window. "It is only Baistrocchi, to whom you listen every day. Now I listen to you. Your papa and the good priest told me about the birthday spinet. I have come with another present—the offer of lessons."

"Maestro!" was all Giuseppe could say.

Luigia Verdi ran to the window to invite the Maestro to supper. He accepted, and they all sat down for a cheerful birthday celebration.

At the table, Giuseppe unwrapped the priest's brown paper parcel. When he found a book of organ selections and Mozart sonatas that the priest had laboriously copied himself, Giuseppe's eyes filled with happy tears.

Solemnly the little boy thanked his parents and his friends.

"Maestro, I hope you will never be sorry for promising to teach me." Then turning to the priest, he bowed again, saying "And . . . . . . I shall try to play the music you have given to me, before my next birthday. And you, dear Mama and Papa, I shall try to make you glad for all the good things you have done for me. This is the most happy birthday in all of Italy."

Giuseppe Verdi kept his word, for the most part. But he was a very little boy, after all, and extremely impatient about music. One day, when he could not find a chord he wanted, he began to pound the little spinet fiercely. Angrily he banged on the keys. Then, with tears in his eyes, he shouted, "You have the chord somewhere. You have the chord, why do you hide it from me? Where is it?"

Then, noticing a small hammer with which his father had been mending the leg of a chair, Giuseppe tearfully picked it up and began to pound the spinet.

"Giuseppe Verdi!" roared a voice like thunder. His father knocked the hammer out of Giuseppe's hands with such force that he fell backwards. Stumbling to the floor, he knocked his head against the innocent spinet. With a cry of pain he put his hand up to his ear. Then, seeing his father's face, he burst into tears.

"I'm sorry, Papa, I shall never be any good. I shall never try again to play music—never."

Carlo Verdi did not smile. He did not comfort the little boy, as he had always done before when he was troubled. By this time, Luigia, who had run in to see what was going on, understood. She looked silently at Giuseppe with an unhappy expression on her gentle face.

"Let us sit down," said Carlo Verdi sternly. Sniffling and very much ashamed of himself, Giuseppe sat in the chair his father had mended that morning.

"Now," said his father, "you have done something not only wrong but stupid as well! In the first place, if you do not know enough music to find and play the chords you wish to play, it is not the fault of the spinet. It is because you have not yet learned enough.

"In the second place, there is no work, no profession, which does not require a time of learning and patience. If you have not the character to work patiently, you will never be able to do anything. When you were but four years old, you had the courage and patience to walk all the way to Busseto to hear music. Now, suddenly, you think you have a right to punish the spinet for which your mother gave up many a new shawl, jacket and sandals to help buy for you."

Carlo Verdi looked very stern and yet very sad. He said, "The only way you can ever earn forgiveness is to work harder than ever. That is all I have to say. Come, Luigia." He took his wife's arm. "There are people waiting in the shop. I shall need your help."

Giuseppe was miserable. He cried for a long time. He knew his father was right. Finally, he bit his lip and blinked back the tears. He made a solem vow to himself that he would do as his father said, that he would work harder than ever and learn to be patient.

On Giuseppe's eighth birthday, the same guests were present for the party, and he gave a special concert for the occasion. The incident of the hammer was long forgotten, for Giuseppe had worked very hard and patiently. The most thrilling moment for his parents and friends came when he played his own composition: "A Mountain Melody."

In the next few years, Giuseppe progressed in music as fast as was possible in the little mountain village. By the time he was ten years old, he was church organist at the cathedral.

Unfortunately, however, he had not had the chance to learn subjects other than music. In those days, education was not provided for all children, as later became the custom in many nations. It was far beyond the means of most farmers, innkeepers, and small tradesmen to send their children to school. In Giuseppe's case, the nearest school was three miles away in Busseto. His parents could not afford tuition, nor could they find a way for him to travel back and forth daily.

Then one evening after the father and son had spent the day in Busseto, Carlo Verdi made an important announcement to the family.

"Today, while Giuseppe listened to the music of the vespers, I finished my work early. So I went to see my old friend, Signor Pugnatta, the shoemaker. I told him of our desire for Giuseppe to further his education. We discussed the matter for five minutes, and what do you think?"

"What, Papa, what?" asked Giuseppe eagerly.

"Yes, do tell us, Carlo," urged Luigia. "What is the result of your discussion with Signor Pugnatta?"

"The result," said Carlo, with great enjoyment, "the result is that for three pennies a day, Giuseppe will live in the home of Signor Pugnatta and attend the best school in Busseto! Now, what do you think of that?"

"I think only of how you have accomplished the impossible!" said Luigia.

"I agree with Mama," said Giuseppe. "I can still come to Roncole every Sunday to play for the services. The pennies I receive for this will help."

So, for two years, Giuseppe Verdi attended school in Busseto. There he learned to read, to write, to speak and understand Latin, and he learned something of history and literature.

Each Sunday morning, he walked to Roncole to fulfill his duties as organist of the little church. Each Sunday evening after vespers, he walked back again to Busseto. In addition to this, in order to help his father make the payments to Signor Pugnatta, Giuseppe played for weddings, christenings, sometimes for funerals. He earned enough so that soon he was able to pay the entire fee to Signor Pugnatta.

Shortly before his twelfth birthday, Giuseppe went from door to door, as artists for the church were allowed to do once a year, asking for extra pennies for his services.

It was quite dark. He made a wrong turn, stumbled and fell into a canal of icy water. When he found he could not climb out by himself he was terrified, for the current was swift and pulled at his legs.

"Help!" shouted Giuseppe at the top of his voice. "Help! Please, oh please, somebody help me! I shall be drowned! Help!"

There was not a sound in the cold night air, except for the rushing water of the canal. Desperately, Giuseppe clung to the tufts of vines and rough bricks. If only someone would come along the road! But no one came.

Giuseppe was getting so stiff with cold he could hardly make his fingers grasp the thin strands of the vines. Once more, with every ounce of strength he could muster, he called out again. "Help me please. Help!"

Up on the dark narrow path along the canal, an old, old woman, scarcely able to hear, stopped uncertainly. Was she imagining it or did she hear the voice of a child? No, she often thought she heard voices, ever since the day long ago when she realized she was growing deaf.

But something made her stop again. Surely it was the voice of a frightened child. It seemed to be coming from the canal! The old woman forgot her infirmities. Suddenly, nimble as a child, she ran to the edge of the canal.

Peering over it intently, she called out, "Hallooo! Where are you? Can you see me? Can you hear me? Can you reach my hand? Hallooooo!"

"Halloo! Halloo!" Giuseppe called out. Through the darkness he saw the old woman reaching for him. She looked like an angel! If only he could reach that hand!

The boy made one last desperate effort, clinging to the slippery weeds and ivy with one hand, clutching for the little shriveled fingers with the other. They seemed hopelessly far away, but just as Giuseppe was about to sink back, he felt the tips of the fingers and gripped tightly. Swiftly the old woman braced her knees against the embankment. She thrust her other arm forward just as Giuseppe loosened his grip on the weeds to reach up with his other hand.

After what seemed an endless struggle, the boy was out of the cold water of the canal, sitting safely on the trail.

"Thank you," he gasped, "thank you with all my heart. All I have are these pennies. You are so welcome to them. Please take them. I shall earn more after the services next Sunday. You have saved my life. I could not have held on any longer. The current was about to carry me away."

"Bless you, my son, bless you," said the old lady, not quite understanding but deeply grateful for the few pennies.

After this shattering experience, Giuseppe's twelfth birthday was like a happy dream following a nightmare. That evening, Carlo Verdi made an announcement which meant the biggest change in the life of the young Giuseppe.

"My dear Luigia, my dear son," he said, "I wish to drink to the health of the parents of Giuseppe Verdi, scholar, musician and now, warehouse apprentice to Signor Antonio Barezzi of Busseto."

Luigia looked shocked and somewhat disappointed. Surely Papa Verdi must be joking! Giuseppe looked puzzled. Signor Antonio Barezzi was a wine dealer! It was from him Carlo bought wine which was sold at the inn.

Carlo Verdi smiled again. "Come, come, my dears! It is not that I wish to see our Giuseppe become a dealer in wines that I rejoice! It is because it is a well-paying position which will give Giuseppe plenty of time to devote to his music. Do you not know that besides being a wine dealer, Signor Barezzi is a fine amateur musician? He is president of the Philharmonic Society of Busseto. It is in his home that they meet, for their rehearsals and concerts!"

Giuseppe said with great relief, "I should have known. What a wonderful chance this will be for me! Oh, Papa, how can I ever thank you?"

It was, indeed, a wonderful thing for Giuseppe Verdi to be able to earn his living and stay at the home of Signor Barezzi. For Signor Barezzi was an understanding and clever man. He introduced the young boy to Maestro Ferdinando Provesi, the conductor of the Philharmonic. Maestro Provesi soon became determined that Giuseppe was a genius who should devote his entire life to music.

But, in the meantime, Signor Barezzi had introduced the boy to the canon of the cathedral. The canon, knowing that the boy was very poor but intelligent, wished him to become a priest. So his friends argued over Giuseppe's career until Signor Barezzi saw a wonderful opportunity to settle the question.

Secretly, Signor Barezzi saw that another organist was installed in the little church at Roncole so that Giuseppe was spared the weekly trip. Instead, he could watch and hear the fine organist in the cathedral in Busseto.

One Sunday, this organist was unable to return from a journey in time for the services. In desperation, the canon sent word to Signor Barezzi. And that gentleman slipped thirteen-year-old Giuseppe into the organ loft!

Thrilled by the beautiful tone of the organ, Giuseppe played his own music—music inspired by his home, the mountains, his friends. There was a great sigh of pleasure and peace as the beautiful music filled the cathedral.

Afterward, the canon rushed to find Signor Barezzi. "Thank you! Where did you find anyone so good so quickly?"

Signor Barezzi smiled mischievously and pointed toward the small doorway to the organ loft. Giuseppe was just coming through it.

"It was you?" said the canon to Giuseppe in astonishment. "You!"

"Oh, ... it was not all right?" asked Giuseppe anxiously.

"Of course, of course," answered the canon hastily. "But what was it?" I did not recognize it. Whose music did you play? It was beautiful."

Timidly Giuseppe looked up at the canon. "Why, why, I had no music, so I played . . . ."

Giuseppe hesitated for a moment, afraid the canon might be angry. Then, courageously, he looked the canon squarely in the eyes and told the truth. "Forgive me, sir, there was no music, so I—I tried to put my thoughts of gratitude into music. Forgive me, if I did wrong."

"Wrong?" growled the canon, "wrong? Who said it was wrong? What else could you do? You were asked to play. There was no music. Either you played something from memory which might not have been suitable, or you played extempore. You are the one who must forgive. I have been a fool, yes, a fool."

The canon smiled at Giuseppe warmly. "I mean, boy, I was a fool to try to encourage you to study for anything but music. Take my word for it now. You cannot do better than to study music, to devote your life to it."

So that is how it was that young Giuseppe Verdi began the serious work of his life, complete devotion to the study, the playing, the composing of music. It was the real beginning of his musical career.

One of the very greatest composers of operatic music, Giuseppe Verdi also composed chamber music, drawing-room music, and beautiful sacred music.

He was blessed with recognition for his work in his lifetime. He left his entire fortune to a home for needy, elderly musicians on a beautiful estate not far from the village of Roncole where he was born. He was a noble spirit as well as a wonderful musician.

JOHANNES BRAHMS

One spring afternoon in the year 1838, a fair-haired boy of five ran through the cobblestone streets of the waterfront in Hamburg, Germany. Even in his clumsy wooden shoes, he darted in and out, skillfully dodging horses and wagons, fishermen, sailors and street vendors. Suddenly he stopped, and a look of delight spread over his face.

To himself he was saying, "It's a song! It's a song! And it sings! It sings and it pounds! And it beats! It's a song!"

He stood in the center of the busy street. There were shouts from every side. A heavy wagon thundered toward him. The driver strained at the reins, unable to stop the horses.

"Hey! Little boy! Jump!"

But the little boy stood still.

In another moment he felt himself being lifted off his feet, as if he were flying through the air. Why, he was in his father's arms, at the side of the street. How did this come about? Little Johannes Brahms was completely surprised.

"Papa! What happened? Papa, I didn't see you."

"No, Johannes. You didn't see anything. Why did you stop like that in the middle of the street? Do you know you were almost run over?" Herr Brahms wiped his forehead.

"Are you all right, Papa?" the boy asked.

Johann Jakob Brahms looked at his little boy's anxious face and laughed gently. "Am *I* all right? What a question! You are the one who was almost run over. It is fortunate I happened to be here. Why did you not jump when that driver called to you?"

"I did not hear him, Papa. I was listening to the song!"

"The song! What song?"

The child smiled happily. "The song of the waterfront, Papa. Horses' hoofs on the cobblestones. People calling—'Fish . . . fresh fish . . . apples, potatoes! Ships' bells—ding, dong, ding! Wagon wheels and wooden shoes—clatter, clatter! It's a song, Papa!"

Herr Brahms looked at Johannes thoughtfully. "Hmm, I see. But, Johannes, you must promise never again to stop in the middle of the street to listen to the song it sings."

"But, Papa——"

"No, Johannes! Promise! I mean it!"

"Yes, Papa," said the boy.

Johannes followed his father through the dingy courtyard of a tall old tenement house, into a first-floor room. He looked longingly at the big box of lead soldiers in the corner. Something told him this was no time to ask if he could play with them.

Then, through the open window, he saw a blossom on a scraggly little bush. He forgot everything else and ran to look. In a minute he was singing at the top of his voice:

> Oh, Spring is here and it is good
> To sing of flowers in the greenwood,
> Of fields and meadows far away
> Where children dance and laugh and play.

"Johannes," said Herr Brahms, "where did you learn that melody?"

"Oh, that is something that sang itself to me. Everything sings to me all the time," the boy said. "There is always music in the air. Of course, I listen every time you play music, Papa. But that is not what I mean."

His father looked thoughtful. He said, "Yes, yes, I know. This is different. You are singing, and quite well, about something you have never seen—the countryside. It is remarkable."

Herr Brahms knew a true musician when he found one, for he was a good musician himself. Indeed, he had struggled to become one, when his own father had said, "Music, nonsense! You must be an innkeeper, like me!"

Now Herr Brahms sometimes wondered if it would not be better for his family if he *were* an innkeeper instead of a musician. So little money came in from the concerts and dancing parties at which he played! His good wife had to help out by sewing for other women. Yet there was barely enough to live on.

"I think it is time for my music lesson, Papa," said little Johannes from the window. He waited eagerly for that time each day. Already he could play viola, flute, violin and horn. He longed to learn to play the piano, now, but the Brahms family had no piano.

"Will we ever have a piano, Papa?" Johannes asked.

"About that, I do not know," said his father. "But I have good news for you. Our neighbor is away on a trip, and he has told me we may use his instrument. So come, child, you shall learn today how to recognize the notes on the piano."

Happily, Johannes ran after his father to the neighboring apartment. His father then played the notes of the scale on the piano and asked Johannes if he could tell him what they were.

"Oh, yes, Papa." Johannes sang out the names of each note correctly without even looking at the piano. He was gazing out the window!

Then Herr Brahms realized that Johannes had the rare gift of absolute pitch.

That day the two of them made another discovery —that Johannes could already play the piano from what he had learned of the viola and violin. Joyously, he played. Soon he was playing melodies his father had never even heard, songs of his own making.

"I love to compose, Papa," he said over and over again. "I would like to compose all the time—if I did not like to play the instruments, too! Papa, I have made up a way to show how the notes of music look on paper, to match the way they sound in my head. See!"

He showed his father how he had worked out a way of putting music on paper. The father looked at five-year-old Johannes in wonder. For the boy's method was one that had been used by musicians for hundreds of years!

Herr Brahms wondered and admired; but he shook his head at Johannes' dream of composing. "You must forget about that, my son," he said. "Composing brings a living to very few. Learn to play the piano properly and well. That is a good trade. You will have to help me earn a living for all of us. Later, you will have to earn a living for yourself.

"Never will I close the doors of music to you, as my father did to me. But music is a hard master. It will take time, hard work, practice and study. And money!" he added, shaking his head again. "Money, indeed. Somehow we must scrape together enough money for piano lessons from a good teacher. Herr Cossel, I think. He is a fine pianist who could teach you far better than I can."

Herr Cossel agreed to teach Johannes after the boy started to school. He was delighted to have such a gifted, intelligent child for his pupil. But he too had little sympathy for Johannes' great interest in composing. So the little boy composed in secret.

He told many friends later, "I was always composing—even in the middle of the night, in school. I did it because I had to."

Herr Cossel was a good teacher, and a thorough one. He saw that Johannes learned to play the piano properly. After the boy had mastered all the exercises given him, he was allowed to learn some of the music of the masters: Bach, Beethoven, Haydn and Mozart.

The lessons went well, but times were very hard for the Brahms family. Often there was not enough to buy food, or to heat the shabby rooms where they lived. Johannes began to play the piano parts with his father's band and other groups. Soon he became known in the neighborhood as that little boy who could play for anything from a band concert to a wedding.

But the children at school teased him. "Johannes is a blockhead. He can't do arithmetic. He can't write a letter. All he can do is play the old piano!"

They laughed and teased even more when Johannes would not go with them to play because he had to practice.

Late one night, Herr Brahms heard someone pounding on the door. Sleepily, he called out, "Who is there?"

"Open the door!"

"Why? Who is it? What do you want?"

"Herr Schröder sent me—Schröder's Restaurant. Johannes has to play."

"Johannes!" Frau Brahms sat up in bed. "Johannes is asleep! Besides, the restaurant is no place for a boy to be this time of night!"

"Please, my dear," said Herr Brahms, putting his finger to his mouth, "Shh." Then aloud he cried out, "What will they pay?"

"Two dollars and food," said the voice outside.

By this time, Johannes was wide awake. He looked

at his mother who was almost in tears. He looked at his father, sad and worried.

Then he spoke up. "I know how much you need the money, Papa. Tell the man I'll go."

Frau Brahms saw how miserable her husband was. She thought for a moment, then straightened up proudly.

"It is gentleness and love at home that counts most," she said quietly. "It is character and morals in the family which influence a child, not outside surroundings. I am not afraid for Johannes to go. He will not do anything to make us unhappy, because he already knows what is right and what is wrong. We always shall be proud of our boy.

Herr Brahms kissed his wife gently and turned to Johannes.

"I will go with you, son," he whispered. Then he called through the door, "It is agreed! We shall be there in five minutes."

So Johannes Brahms began at the age of seven to help support his family. Every night, he played the piano somewhere, for something. It was hard work, for he practiced many hours a day, read everything he could, and went to school as well.

Johannes enjoyed the music and the books. But still he dreamed of the day he would have the time and permission to compose. He wanted with all his heart to study with a teacher who would let him compose.

"There must be something else I can do," he kept telling himself, "to make more money."

Then, one day in school, he had an idea. He was so excited he could hardly wait to get home and tell his father. That day, some boys ran after him, teasing again. Johannes tried not to listen. He had something much more important to think about. Faster and faster he ran. When he reached the busy waterfront, he darted in and out among the wagons and carriages, running like the wind.

Suddenly he slipped and fell. There were screams and shouts, the whinnying and neighing of horses, and then a terrible silence. The boys who had followed Johannes from school looked frightened. The driver of the wagon that had hit Johannes jumped down angrily.

To the boys he shouted, "You see what you did, you rascals, chasing this poor little fellow into the street like that. See now, the wheel ran right over him, it did. You know him? You know where he lives? Lead me there, you rascals! Hurry up now. This boy is hurt!"

Silently the children led the way to the courtyard apartment near the waterfront.

Frau Brahms, worried as she was, comforted the

other children and nursed Johannes until the doctor came. Herr Brahms arrived just as the little boy was being examined by the solemn-faced doctor.

"This is very serious," the doctor said. "One wheel ran over the boy's chest. The child is small and not very strong. We must be careful that he is not moved any more than necessary. He must have plenty of rest and good food. Then we shall see. We shall see."

Johannes opened his eyes and smiled. "Papa. Mama. It was not anybody's fault. It was because I was hurrying home to tell you . . . to tell you. . . ."

"Tell us what, son?" asked his father.

"Shh. No questions," said the doctor.

So it was several days before Herr Brahms found out what had made Johannes want to hurry home.

The boy surprised him by saying, "I will be all right soon. I have to be! Because I am going to earn money for lessons with the great Professor Marxsen. You will help, Papa. We will have a concert."

"A concert! Who?" asked the father.

"You and I and your sextet. The men who play in the sextet are all good musicians. It will be a fine concert. We will charge admission. We will tell everyone we are raising money for me to study with a great master!"

When Herr Brahms looked uncertain, Johannes begged, "Papa, please say yes!"

Frau Brahms like the idea. "Jakob," she said to her husband, "I think Johannes is quite right. He might play the piano, part of the Beethoven wind quintet you and your friends play so nicely, and perhaps an étude. . . . ."

"Yes, Mama, that would be good! Please, Papa?"

"Johannes, my boy, I agree! It is a splendid idea. Though I wonder if enough people would attend to fill the concert pavillion! Well first, you must get well. That is the most important thing of all."

"I'll get well in a hurry now," said the boy. "I wish the doctor would let me practice! But he says I have to stay in bed."

"Yes, Johannes dear, and Mama is right here to follow the doctor's orders," said Frau Brahms.

"*I know what!*" shouted Johannes.

"Shh," said his mother. "Remember what the doctor said. No shouting until we are sure the lungs and the chest are quite healed. Now, tell us quietly. What have you thought up now?"

"A way to practice. If Papa will get me a big piece of cardboard I can make a dummy keyboard. Then I can practice right here in bed. Lying down. Hmm? How about that, Papa?"

"That is an excellent plan if the doctor agrees."

"And to that the doctor does agree," said the doctor himself as he came in the door to make his call.

"It will keep our young, hard-working genius busy in a nice quiet way. But not until next week, you need a few more days of absolute quiet. But with this to look forward to, and your mother to read to you, it will not be hard. This copy of *Swiss Family Robinson* is waiting to be read."

For six long weeks, Johannes "practiced" on his dummy keyboard. Six long weeks it was before he was able to get out of bed. But he did get well, and he did have the concert. It was a great success. A visiting concert-manager offered to take Johannes and all his family on a concert tour of Europe and the United States. But Johannes' piano teacher, Herr Cossel, was horrified at the idea.

"The boy has not yet completed his musical training," he said. "A concert tour, when he is not ready —Unthinkable! It might ruin his work. He must study more, with a good master, as he has wanted to do. Will you refuse this concert tour, Herr Brahms, if Professor Marxsen will agree to guide Johannes from now on?"

"There is no money for such lessons except what we raised in the concert," said Herr Brahms with a sigh. "When that is gone. . ."

"Then we shall see," said Herr Cossel happily. Quickly he hurried to Professor Marxsen and told the story of what had happened. At last the great master agreed to undertake the education of young Johannes. He would teach the boy harmony, sight transposing, counterpoint and composition, while Herr Cossel continued his training in piano.

So the work began, and Johannes was happy. For now at last he could compose. Maybe his dream would come true some day!

But as the years passed, times were harder than ever for the poor Brahms family. More and more often did Johannes have to help by playing at night, sometimes all night, always for two dollars. But Johannes had his books. Each night, he propped a book up on the piano and between dances he read. Never did he neglect his practicing. Always he had his school work.

Herr Brahms began to watch him anxiously. He became more and more alarmed, as he saw how pale and thin the boy was growing.

He thought, "Johannes needs the fresh pure air of the country. I wonder how we can manage it."

He went to see Adolph Giesemann, a wealthy music-lover who lived in Winsen, sixty miles from Hamburg. Herr Giesemann had often heard Johannes play, and had praised him every time.

That night, Herr Brahms came home happy with good news.

"Listen, everyone! Our Johannes is going to get

well and strong again. No more night work for a whole summer! Johannes is invited to spend the summer on the country estate of Herr Giesemann! He will have no duties except to give lessons to Herr Giesemann's little daughter. Once a week, Johannes will come to Hamburg for his own music lessons."

It was a happy boy who joined Herr Giesemann to travel into the country. His eyes took in everything as they drove through the countryside. Never had he seen anything like the rolling fields, the beautiful woods, the streams, the flowers and trees!

"It sings," he said to himself over and over again. "It's beautiful music and it sings!"

Herr Giesemann smiled as he watched the excited boy. Every day on the Giesemann estate, Johannes ran to look at every flower, every tree. Always he found something new and heard new music in the air, all through the summer. He saw birds' nests and robins' eggs, butterflies and wild roses. Things he had never seen before in his thirteen years in the city.

He had time to read and to practice and to write down the music the countryside sang to him. He went to a concert, just to listen. That seemed wonderful to him, too—to be able to sit and listen, instead of playing the music.

Johannes spent much of every day out of doors, and his health rapidly improved. He liked Herr

Geisemann and the whole family; he liked Lischen, the daughter to whom he gave lessons on the piano. Life in the country was perfect.

Every morning, Johannes woke up at dawn and went for a swim in the river. Before anyone else was up, he wrote down some new music, practiced on his dummy keyboard, or walked in the woods.

He played accompaniments for Herr Giesemann and for the men's chorus of Winsen. He gave a lesson each day to Lischen, and walked for endless miles over the beautiful countryside.

By the end of the summer, Johannes was well and strong again and completely happy. That autumn he played in two Hamburg recitals and secretly felt hope that his dream might come true. He would have time to compose. But again he had to play for restaurants and dances almost every night during the school year.

Happily, he was invited to spend the next summer in Winsen. This time it seemed even more wonderful, and he composed more than he had before. One morning, Johannes showed Lischen a big pile of music.

"What is it, Johannes?" she asked.

"It's music I wrote last night."

"Last night! All that?"

"Yes, it's not hard. It comes into my head, and I

write it down, that's all. Lischen, this is music I wish the Winsen Choral Society would use. It is a song especially for them. Do you think they would like such a thing—from me?"

"Oh yes, Johannes! Yes!" said Lischen. "That is wonderful! Wait till I tell Father!"

Herr Giesemann was pleased, too. And the Winsen Choral Society used that song by Johannes for more than one hundred years.

That fall of 1848, when Brahms was fifteen years old, he gave a concert of his own in which he played a Bach fugue. His teachers were pleased and proud of him and took him to hear the famous Hungarian violinist Joseph Joachim. Johannes thought he had never heard anything so beautiful.

All too soon, Johannes was back again in the hopeless world of work—trying to study hard and make money at the same time. Soon he was playing for the city theater of Hamburg, as well as all the other places. Still there was not enough money to provide for all the needs of his family. What more could he do? Johannes began to give piano lessons.

For three years he had never a minute, it seemed, to compose. By the time he was eighteen, he had decided that he must remain forever in Hamburg, teaching all day, playing all night, and composing only once in a great while.

Then something happened to change his whole life. The Hungarian gypsy violinist, Remenyi, heard Johannes play, and asked him to be his accompanist in a Hamburg concert. The violinist was delighted with Johannes' work at that concert. At once he wanted the young man to play for him on a long tour.

Johannes could hardly believe that he was not dreaming. On a concert tour he would be free to compose much of the time; yet he would earn enough to continue helping at home. No more playing nights—he would play on the concert stage, with an important artist! It seemed too good to be true.

He almost shouted in his eagerness. "Yes! I'll go. I'll do it. Just let me tell my family, and I shall be ready."

And family and friends were happy to hear of Johannes' good fortune. The Brahmses had a celebration, and sent Johannes off with many good wishes. His mother put a small sewing kit in his pocket. "To keep the buttons on the best you can," she said.

The tour with Remenyi was a great success. During it, Johannes met Joseph Joachim, the violinist he had admired so much, years before. The two musicians became fast friends, and Joachim arranged for Johannes to meet the great composer, Schumann.

Kindly, politely, Schumann talked with young Brahms, and asked him to play something. Trembling, he began his *Sonata in C Major*.

Almost at once, the great Schumann said, "Stop!" Johannes looked up unhappily, but there was no disappointment on Schumann's gentle face. "Clara must hear this!" he said, and called to his wife.

In a moment, Clara Schumann came into the room. Johannes stood up and bowed shyly. She was a musician herself, one of Europe's finest pianists.

"Now, my dear Clara," Robert Schumann said, "listen to such as you have never heard before!"

As Schumann said those words, Johannes Brahms truly heard music. It was like an overture, a beautiful beginning to something important. It was a promise of hope that he could make his dream come true, and still help his family. Before his slim young fingers touched the keys again, he bowed his head.

That night, Schumann wrote in his diary, "Herr Brahms from Hamburg to see me——(a genius!)"

The hardest days were over. Johannes Brahms had packed a lifetime of struggle and hard work into nineteen years. Now, he was on his way. Always, he did his best. His devotion to music was untiring through many more busy years. No other musician of his time gave more fine music to the world.

PETER ILICH TCHAIKOVSKY

On May 7, 1840, just when the winter snows were melting in the great open Russian countryside, Peter Ilich Tchaikovsky was born. His family was well-to-do and music-loving, and the little boy had unusual talent, yet Peter grew up without seriously studying music. This odd fact is true of no other famous composer, and many people have wondered how it could have happened.

When Peter was four years old, the older children in the family—a brother and two girl cousins—were beginning their education. They had a governess whom they all liked, and Peter wanted to join them.

"Please, please, please let me. Why can't I, Papa?" Peter begged so earnestly his father laughed and picked him up for a toss in the air.

"Well, ask Mama to explain that you are too young to start lessons. You might hold the other children back."

"But if I promise not to? If I work even harder than they do, will you let me?"

Peter spoke so seriously that his father at last conceded, "Well, we shall leave it all to your mother. Whatever she says, goes."

"Mama! You heard what Papa said! Please, Mama, please!"

Peter's mother looked over at Miss Anna, the governess, and they both laughed.

"What do you think, Madame Tchaikovsky?" asked Anna.

"My dear Anna, it is up to you. If it is not too much for you, and if Peter does not hold back the others, I see no reason why he should not join in the lessons."

"Mama!" shouted Peter happily. "And that means music lessons, too?"

"Why, Peter!" said Madame Tchaikovsky. "I had no idea it was music you wanted to study. I thought, of course, it was reading and writing."

"Oh," added Peter hastily, for fear he would lose his chance, "I mean reading and writing, too, but music, music for certain. You and Miss Anna play, and the others are learning to play. Please, Mama!"

"Well, Peter, dear," said Madame Tchaikovsky, "it will be difficult for you to reach the pedals with your feet and the keys with those little hands of yours all at the same time. But you have my permission to try, my darling."

From the very beginning, the lessons for Peter with the older children worked out beautifully. He kept up with them in the reading, writing, and language studies so that he could study music. In that he surpassed them all.

Every day when the lessons were over, Peter's older brother and his cousins ran off to watch the men surveying and constructing at the mines, but not Peter! He stayed close to Miss Anna, learning all the music he could find in the house. He loved stories, too. He begged Miss Anna for stories even when he was able to read them himself.

After he heard the story of "The Snow Maiden" for the first time, he asked for it over and over. Finally he knew the tale so well that he would often tell it to Miss Anna.

"It is sad and happy too, Miss Anna," he said, one afternoon. "That's why I like it."

Anna gave Peter a loving hug.

"It is, indeed, Peter Ilich Tchaikovsky! And you tell it far better than I do. It sounds like music when you tell of the little Snow Maiden. And speaking of music, it is now lesson time. Would you like to play something for me before we begin?"

"How did you know, Miss Anna? Because I

would! I would like to play something I have been thinking about since you first told me the story about the Snow Maiden."

When Peter finished, Miss Anna was so quiet, Peter bit his lips to keep back the tears.

"You do not like it, Miss Anna?"

"Oh Peter, I do! I like it very much. The melody is beautiful. I was trying to remember when you had learned it, and where. It is not one I have taught you, nor has your mother, I think."

"No, Miss Anna, it is not! I am so glad you like it. I hoped you would, because it is the melody that sings to me inside of my head whenever you tell about how Peter and Anna heard music when the little Snow Maiden played in their garden."

Miss Anna looked very thoughtful for a moment and then she said, "Peter Ilich Tchaikovsky, I think you should begin studying music with someone who knows more about it than I do. That was a beautiful melody and so are others I have heard you play. There is only one thing I question. They all sound rather sad. Are you sad, Peter?"

"Oh, no, Miss Anna," Peter protested. "How could I be sad? I am happy. I have music and stories, and I love you and all my family!"

Miss Anna was relieved. But she worried about Peter because he was quieter than most children. He dreamed too much, perhaps—was too fond of make-believe. But he was really happy in those days.

It was not until after his father's work took the family to the great city of St. Petersburg that Peter began to understand the meaning of what Miss Anna had said about unhappiness. As was the custom among wealthy families, Peter's parents sent him to a boarding school when he was only eight years old. The school discipline was strict, hours were long, and Peter seldom saw his family. Worst of all, his parents believed that he had had enough music now. It was time to learn important things.

One evening, Peter was lying in bed wide awake, long after lights were out, feeling lonely and very unhappy. He had felt this way a long time now, for he had been at school several years. Suddenly, from far off down the street, he heard the music of a hand organ. As it came closer, he recognized an old Russian folk song which he had played and sung at home many times. He listened, enraptured, and when the music was right outside, he jumped out of bed and ran to the window. There he watched and listened until the organ grinder disappeared in the distance.

"Music!" he said to himself. "If I had music, it would be different here." He thought of the piano, and the practice room. "Everyone else is asleep. No one can hear me if I close the door . . ."

Peter tiptoed down the steps, opened the door into the dark, unused practice room, and found his way to the piano. Silently he fingered the keys. How good they felt! For some reason he thought of the little melody he had played for Miss Anna. He began to play it softly, making up variations on the theme as he went along.

He did not hear any footsteps. He did not hear the door. But suddenly, he saw before him a very astonished-looking gentleman, in night shirt and night cap.

"What is going on in here?" the man asked, rubbing his eyes. Was this really a frightened little boy, shivering in his night shirt, looking small and lonely at the big piano? Professor Phillipov came closer. Squinting his eyes, he peered intently into Peter's face, holding his fluttering candle high.

"Peter Ilich Tchaikovsky, is that you?"

"Yes, sir. Excuse me, sir. I am very sorry if I wakened you. I did not mean to waken anybody. Is it Professor Phillipov? I cannot see very well in the dark."

"No, neither can I," muttered Professor Phillipov. "And who can, for that matter? They say cats can, but how do we know that? How can we tell?"

"I really don't know, sir," answered Peter, trying not to laugh. "Excuse me, sir, I am very sorry."

"Humph," grunted the Professor. "Yes, you are right, Peter. It is I, Professor Phillipov. But the middle of the night is no time for discipline. Oh, Peter Ilich Tchaikovsky, how could I scold you anyway, when you play such beautiful music? All I can say is this: Play it again, child! See if you can remember how you did it—but softly, boy, softly."

"Yes, sir. I am so glad you like it, sir. I am not sure I can do it in exactly the same way, but this is the idea. It is based on an old folk song."

Professor Phillipov came closer to the piano with his candle held high so he could see Peter better. The tassel of the Professor's white night cap bobbed up and down as he kept time with his head, his free arm swinging gently like a baton.

Peter was enchanted. This was the most fun he had had in this boarding school. At the same time, the unexpected kindness of Professor Phillipov made him so grateful he put his feelings into the music as he played.

Peter thought fiercely to himself. "What makes me feel like crying, anyway? I will not cry! I will not!"

Professor Phillipov knew boys well enough to sense something of what was going through Peter's mind. Gently, he put his hand on the boy's thin shoulder.

"What is it?" he asked. "Something troubles you, Peter. Your music is beautiful, though very sad. If you continue in this way, it will break both our hearts. Thank you for playing it again. Tell me, Peter, what is in your mind, as you play?"

When he saw the look of sympathy and understanding in the Professor's eyes, Peter poured forth his thoughts, freely, as he always had done at home. It was wonderful to be able to talk to someone who was interested. Peter, always shy with strangers, forgot that Professor Phillipov was a teacher and poured out his heart.

"Oh, Professor Phillipov! For one thing, I am afraid I shall never be a good lawyer, as my parents want me to be. I try, and I get along well enough to pass, but I am not really interested, not one bit. I keep closing the book and hearing music. Yet I do not think I play so very well."

"I think you do," said Professor Phillipov.

"Not the way I hear in my head how it should be played," said Peter. "But I love music so much!"

"Do your parents know this?" asked the Professor.

"Yes, they know how I love music," said Peter. "And they have given me some lessons with a very good teacher. Until now, that is. But—well, I am not a good enough musician for my father to think I can give up everything else for music. He wants me to study for the law. He thinks I can earn a better living that way. What shall I do, Professor Phillipov? What shall I do?"

Professor Phillipov put his hand reassuringly on the boy's shoulder. As if the boy were a grown man, he considered what Peter had said. "Peter, let me tell you what I think you should do, while you are here in school, anyway. Beginning tomorrow, we shall add music to your studies. I shall teach you all I can. Each day you shall have a lesson. Each day you may practice as much as you like after your other lessons are prepared. In this way you can learn a great deal by yourself."

"Thank you!" Peter exclaimed.

Then he looked solemn as the Professor continued, "You are a very young boy, so now you must study what your father wishes, but it will be good for you to study the courses needed for law school. It will train your mind, broaden your knowledge, make you a better musician if you should become one later on. In this way, you will please your father and study the music so necessary to your happiness. And some day perhaps he, and others, too, will understand that you have a real talent."

He smiled at Peter. "Now, run back to bed before you catch cold; but run very quietly. I have no desire to report this interview to the headmaster!"

Peter slipped off the piano bench, bowed solemnly and politely, and fervently whispered to this wonderful man, "Thank you, Professor Phillipov, thank you with all my heart. I shall never forget this."

For years after that conversation at school, Peter worked hard to please his parents. He loved them, and he hated arguments and scenes. He would do almost anything to keep from fighting with his parents.

He graduated from the School of Jurisprudence, and went to work as a law clerk for the government.

But all through this time he longed for more music. He did manage to find some room for it in his life, so that he was never completely without it any more. He joined singing societies, took lessons in composition, and practiced piano, after working hours.

When he was busy with his job as a law clerk, he approached a famous music master, who consented to hear him play. Maestro Zaremba listened, smiled, asked a question or two, and listened again.

"Now improvise for me," the master said.

Peter improvised on the old folk tune that he loved and had played for Professor Phillipov.

Then Maestro Zaremba said, "You are a musician, young man. You know much of composition . . . beautiful harmonies . . . melodies! But there is always more to learn. We shall begin tomorrow!"

Although Peter had to keep his job in order to pay for the lessons, Maestro Zaremba was delighted with his progress. Peter began to spend every free moment studying and practicing in the conservatory. At last, in 1863, when Peter Ilich Tchaikovsky was twenty-three years old, he gave up everything to become a full-time student at the conservatory.

Peter did not let the embarrassment of being older than the other students, or the life of poverty he was forced to live, stand in his way. He studied feverishly, learned everything he could about every phase of music.

When he was twenty-five, Peter finished his courses. The very next year, he was offered the post of Professor of Harmony in the new conservatory in Moscow.

It was a happy day for the world, for children and grownups, when Peter Ilich Tchaikovsky had the courage to foresake a comfortable living as a law clerk at the age of twenty-three, and start all over again in music.

No lovelier music for children has ever been written than the music of Peter Tchaikovsky. He wrote music for his old favorite, "The Snow Maiden." *The Nutcracker* and the *Sleeping Beauty* ballet music are favorites everywhere.

Tchaikovsky is known also for his symphonies,

violin and piano concertos, overtures, and much ballet music.

Today there is a difference of opinion among critics about the quality of his music. But even his severest critics agree that it is beautiful.

PART II
COMPOSERS OF AMERICA

STEPHEN FOSTER

On July 4, 1826—the fiftieth birthday of the United States—Stephen Foster was born. In those days, people held even greater celebrations on the Fourth of July than they do today. All-day outings were the rule, with picnics and speeches and bands, as well as fireworks. Little Stephen's birthday made the day a double holiday for the Foster family.

On his second birthday, in 1828, the Fosters were preparing for a picnic. Everyone was in the kitchen except Stevie. He was too little to help—but where was he? Sister Ann Eliza went to search for him.

When she found her baby brother, she gazed at him in great surprise. Then she ran back to the kitchen to the others.

"Mama! William, Morrison, Charlotte! Everybody! Come and look. Stevie is playing the guitar."

"What?" Mrs. Foster jumped up quickly from the table where she was wrapping sandwiches. "Why, it was high out of his reach. How would he get it?"

"He can climb," said his big brother William. "But I did not know he could play the guitar, too. I've seen him playing Mama's melodeon when he thought he was alone. He sings. Pretty good music, too."

Mrs. Foster looked at her oldest son in amazement. "Stevie was at my melodeon? Playing the organ and singing?"

Now it was the turn of Lieve, the young Negro girl who worked for the Fosters. "Oh yes, ma'am. I've heard him, too," she said. "Stevie loves to sing. He knows all the hymns in my hymnbook. And when I take him to church with me, he sings better than anyone else."

"But he's only two years old," said Mrs. Foster. "He can hardly talk."

"Well, that makes no matter," said Lieve. "That child is full of music. He is just made for music."

"Come and see him now," said Ann Eliza.

She led the way into the parlor on tip-toe, and cautioned the others to be quiet.

Stevie was a sight to see. He knelt on the floor in front of the big guitar. By this time, he had found the first part of a melody he wanted. Now he was struggling with the rest of it. He plucked the strings with one hand. As he found each note of the tune, he smiled with delight.

"I know!" whispered Ann Eliza. "He's playing that song Lieve sings so much: 'Git on board, little children, there's room for many-a more!' "

"That's right, he is," whispered Lieve. She began to hum as Stevie plucked the guitar strings.

Stevie looked up and smiled, but he kept right on playing. "Little pianni?" he said.

Everyone laughed.

"No, not a little piano!" said Ann Eliza. "It's a guitar, Stevie. And you play beautiful music on it. Good for Stevie."

"Good for Stevie," the little boy echoed.

From that time on, he played the guitar every day, sitting with it on the floor or at a table until he was big enough to hold the instrument. It was not long before he could play any piece he liked.

When his sister Charlotte's friend came to spend the summer, she had her own piano sent from home so that she could practice.

Stevie spent hours at that piano. He tried to play everything he heard, and after a few tries he could do so, no matter what the music was.

Charlotte's friend was impressed with the little boy's talent, and she spoke to the family about it. "He is so gifted," she said. "Don't you think he should have a piano?"

"I certainly do not," said Mr. Foster sternly.

Everybody looked at him in surprise, especially his wife. "Well, of course, it would be expensive," she said. "Actually we could not afford it now, but later perhaps, if I were to save a bit here and there. I can see no harm in it."

"I can," said Mr. Foster gruffly. "Do we want a lazy musician in the family?"

"Papa!" said Charlotte. She looked anxiously at her friend, who had just told them she wished to become a musician. But the girl laughed good-naturedly.

"Lots of American men feel that way," she said. "But in France, where my mother comes from, they don't. Mama has persuaded my father to look upon the arts in the European way. Papa is now convinced that if anyone has a talent he should use it rather than work at something he doesn't like and isn't good at. Papa says people do better and go farther that way and end up happier."

"Humph!" growled Mr. Foster. And he adjusted his steel-rimmed spectacles and turned back to his newspaper.

Mrs. Foster and the older girls busied themselves with the tea tray, trying to cover up the embarrassed silence.

But William laughed heartily and reached out his hand. "Good for your Father," he said to Charlotte's friend. "I'd like to meet him. And I certainly do agree with you. Stevie *should* have a piano!"

One day, after the visitor had gone, a big wagon pulled up to the Fosters' back door. Two men climbed down and began to unload a huge wooden crate.

"What is it? What is it?" Stevie jumped up and down with excitement. Not many packages like that were delivered to the Foster house!

"Well, where does she go?" asked the driver, at the kitchen door.

Lieve stopped her work and jumped to attention.

"Oh, yes, where does she go? What? Where does who go?"

"The piano! What did you think?" said the driver impatiently. "Hurry up, please—we have another delivery to make."

"Oh! Oh, yes, excuse me," said Lieve. "Oh, I must ask Mrs. Foster."

"I will!" shouted Stevie. "Mama! Somebody's coming to visit Charlotte again. Somebody with a piano. Where shall they put it? Mama!"

Mrs. Foster came into the kitchen. "No one is coming to visit, Stevie. Please put it in the parlor, driver. Lieve, show the gentleman in and see that he puts it where we had the piano when Miss Charlotte's friend was here."

"Yes, ma'am," said Lieve, smiling broadly.

Stevie's eyes were shining. He could hardly wait until the piano was uncrated.

"What happened, Mama?" he asked. "Why did they bring a piano here?"

"Stevie dear, this is a gift to you from your brother William. He has been doing extra work at everything he could find, to earn the money for it. Now what do you think of that?"

Stevie could not answer. He was too happy to talk. When the piano was in place, he ran to it, climbed up on the stool, and began to play. He looked completely happy.

Life was a joyful thing to Stevie. When he started to school, he enjoyed that, too. He liked the small town of Harmony, Pennsylvania, where he lived. He liked to play out of doors and ride his pony. Best of all, he liked to go to the little church with Lieve on Sunday evenings. He loved the hymns the Negro people sang, and the way they sang. He loved the sound of their beautiful voices.

Harmony was a river town, and Stevie was glad of that, too. Down at the river wharf, where the boats and barges unloaded, he could hear more music. The boatmen sang as they worked, and they knew songs Stevie had never heard before. He went to the wharf almost every day after school, to listen and learn. And he longed to take a trip on the river, a trip to the South, where the boatmen said he could hear still more songs.

He did go south on the river, on a trip with his mother. Joyfully, he made up a song about sailing down the river. "We're sailing down the river," he sang. "The river, the river! We're sailing down the river, the Oh-hi-o!"

For a week, Stephen and his mother visited in a little town of Kentucky. Here Stevie learned more of the Negro music he loved so much. He went with the Negroes to the cotton fields where they worked, to their cabins where they sang and danced after the day's work, and to their churches where he worshiped and sang with them. He remembered every melody he heard in Kentucky, and all the things the people did. They adored the little boy, and he loved them.

Once, visiting in the city of Pittsburgh, Stevie and his mother were taking a walk. Eagerly he looked in every shop window. All of a sudden, he stopped in front of one window and would not move on.

"Oh, Mama, look!"

The window was filled with musical instruments. Stevie impulsively ran into the store and picked up a flute from a counter. He began to play it in pure, singing tones. Soon there was a cluster of admiring strangers around him.

Stevie smiled but did not really see them. He lifted the flute again and played a song he had heard the Negroes singing in Kentucky.

Mrs. Foster began to be nervous. A gentleman who seemed to be in charge of the store was walking up to her little boy. When Stevie finished the melody, she stepped forward and spoke to him quite firmly.

"Stevie," she said, "you have no right to pick up an instrument which does not belong to you, or to play it without asking permission. It is very bad manners."

Stevie stammered, "I—I didn't think. It is such a lovely flute. I wish. . . . "

"No," said his mother, guessing his wish. "You already have a piano and a guitar."

She turned to the strange gentleman who now stood next to them. "I am very sorry, sir. Please forgive my little boy. He just picked up the flute without thinking."

"Madam," said the gentleman, bowing politely, "my name is Henry Kleber. I am a music teacher, not the store manager."

To Stevie he said, "My boy, you are quite a musician! A very good one, indeed. Who is your teacher?"

"I have no teacher, sir," said Stevie. "Doesn't the

flute have a beautiful sound? It is a very nice one, isn't it?"

Mr. Kleber looked at Mrs. Foster with a puzzled expression. "Am I to understand this boy has never played a flute before?"

"No, never. He has played a guitar and piano. That is all."

"Without a teacher?" asked Mr. Kleber.

"Without a teacher," said Mrs. Foster.

Mr. Kleber exclaimed, "Madam, it is unbelievable! I have never seen anything like it! Maybe in Europe, where music is encouraged, but here in the new world, no! Madam, the boy should have lessons."

"We do not live here," said Mrs. Foster, more and more embarrassed in front of the smiling crowd. Stevie was having such a good time, she really did not want to spoil it, but still . . . She thought of her husband, and how he felt about music for Stevie. What would he say to this adventure?

Mr. Kleber tipped his hat to her and patted Stevie on the shoulder. Then he tapped the flute that was still in the boy's hands.

"Take it, lad," he said, "take it. It will be my pleasure to make you a gift of this flute. Enjoy it—and see that you always play it so well!"

"Oh, thank you, sir," said Stevie. He thought Mr. Kleber was the nicest man he had ever met.

"If we lived in this city, I would like to take music lessons from you, sir!"

Mrs. Foster and Stevie left, to the applause of the little group around them,

That evening, when Stevie played on his new flute, his father nodded absently. "Yes, yes, you play well, of course. But music, my son, is not to be the work of your life. You must begin to think far more seriously about your studies."

"Yes, Papa," said Stevie. "I do my lessons, Papa."

As he looked out on the busy street, he lifted his flute, and began to play a lively, gay, rollicking tune of his own. He was thinking, "I can take a flute with me everywhere. Like the old lady with rings on her fingers and bells on her toes, I can have music wherever I go. Yes, a flute is the best thing to have."

The flute and Stevie were together all the time after that. When the children went to see the popular minstrel shows, full of singing and dancing and jokes, Stevie took his flute along. Between acts, he slipped outside to try out the tunes the minstrels had sung.

When the performers paraded down the main street before a show, Stevie Foster followed them—with his flute. When the minstrel shows left town, Stevie felt as if all the joy had disappeared from Harmony. But he comforted himself by playing the minstrel songs on his flute.

Once he organized a show to be given by some of the boys of the town, friends who had seen most of the minstrel shows, too. Stevie taught the other boys the songs and the dances. They practiced the jokes. They cleaned up the Foster stable for the show, and sold tickets all over town.

It was a fine show—just like the professional minstrels, everybody said. Stevie got most of the credit for its success, and he deserved it. Even Mr. Foster said the show was enjoyable, and praised Stevie for his hard work.

"Yes, yes, it was very good," his father said. "And remember this! Just work that hard at a good sensible job and some day everything will be fine."

"Yes, papa, I know," answered Stevie dreamily. "Because when I grow up, I am going to be an actor and a singer. Then I can have music all the time, because in-between performances, I can be writing new songs and learn new stories and dance steps and it will be just wonderful!"

"*Stephen Foster!*" roared his father.

There was a gasp from the whole family. Anxiously they all looked at the little boy.

Stevie's face had turned white. "Yes, Papa?"

"You will do nothing of the kind! An actor! A singer! The life of a minstrel will not be the life of any son of mine, and never forget it!"

"Yes, Papa," said Stevie soberly. To himself he thought, "*Why* does he want me to do something I have no wish to do, when there is something I love more than anything?"

After that, whenever Stevie felt he had to play music, he took his flute into the stable, or into the fields outside the village. He tried very hard to keep himself away from the piano or the guitar when his father was at home, but somehow he managed to play and to sing more than ever.

When Stevie was a little older, Mr. Foster decided that the boy must go away to school. He must concentrate on real study, in a good school—not in a little country school any longer.

"I expect you to give a good account of yourself at Athens Academy, Stevie," Mr. Foster said. "I do not forbid you to find pleasure and recreation with a certain amount of music, if you must. But never play any music until all lessons are well learned and prepared for your next day's classes. Is that clearly understood?"

"Yes, Papa," Stevie answered with a lump in his throat.

"I want your word of honor, Stephen."

"I give you my word, Papa."

With that his father was satisfied.

Stephen's brother William was very kind and

understanding about the big change. He drove Stevie to Tioga Falls, the town where the Academy was. He made the trip a gay and interesting one, trying to help Stevie forget the awful homesickness he already felt.

William found a place for his young brother to stay in Tioga Falls. Then he gave him a sudden hug to say good-by.

At the last moment, he reached into his bag and pulled out a long, narrow package. "Here's something for you, Stevie. It is no piano, of course. But I think you will like it just the same."

When Stevie saw what was in the package, he shouted for joy. "William! A clarinet! Thank you, William. Thank you."

"All right, youngster," said William with a pleased smile. "But don't forget, not a note out of you and Mr. Clarinet before lessons are prepared."

"I won't forget, William!" said Stevie earnestly. "Cross my heart."

"You're a good boy, Stevie. Good-by, and good luck with Latin and all those figures. They're not easy! Not for me, anyway."

"Nor for me," said Stevie ruefully, "but I'll do my best."

"Nobody can do more," shouted William, already on his way.

It was not an easy time for young Stephen Foster, but not an entirely unhappy one. He did work at his lessons so he would have time for music every evening. His biggest sorrow was that he could not afford to attend the special class in music. But the boys who were in the class lent him their books, told him what the assignments were, and he took the course by himself. In this way he learned how to write down the melodies he was always composing for his flute.

In the practice room of the Academy, Stevie was allowed to play the piano when everyone else had finished. It was here one evening that Stevie had an idea.

"I'll do it!" he said to the big empty room. This waltz would be just right for it."

The minute he got to his room, he lighted the candle and began to write, humming and singing as he did so. Once in a while he would get up, play a few notes on the flute, then run back to the table and write a few notes on the paper. Back and forth he went until the candle burned down and in the sky, a light began to appear.

"Oh my goodness," said Stevie, looking at his ink-smudged hands. "It's morning! I must get busy and clean up."

The cold water felt good on his face and Stevie was much too excited to feel tired, sleepy or hungry.

He ran to school as fast as he could. He wanted time to see some friends, who liked to play the flute, too.

One of them was just coming into the classroom. "Look at us!" the boy laughed. "Can't wait to get to school. I have to write a paper all over again. Why are you so early, Stevie?"

"I'll tell you," said Stevie breathlessly. "I was thinking last night, John, about the Spring Celebration exercises next month. Well, I thought it would be nice if you and Joe and I could play something special on our flutes. Of course, it is really for four flutes, but that won't matter too much."

"What is for four flutes?"

Stevie pulled out a roll of music paper. "This."

Just then Joe came in. Luckily, he had his flute with him, too. Stevie showed both boys how the waltz should go. They began to follow him, each playing one of the parts Stephen had written.

"This is good, Stevie," the others said. "Where did you find it? In the library?"

"Oh, no," Stevie said hastily.

"Well, where?" asked John. "It's a good tune, great for a flute."

"Well, I didn't exactly find it. I mean, yes I found it all right but, well, I mean——"

"What's the matter with you?" asked his friends, laughing.

"I mean, I'm glad you like it," said Stevie with a grin, "because I wrote it."

"What do you know about that!" said Joe admiringly. "What do you think of that!"

The boys received permission to play the waltz at the school program. When the day came, the director announced to the big audience, "Our next number will be 'Tioga Waltz,' written for four flutes by Stephen Collins Foster."

The boys had practiced well. They knew their music and liked to play. When they began the "Tioga Waltz" they gave it all the joy and swing and rhythm that Stevie had written into it. The audience liked it so much they applauded until the boys repeated the number.

All during Stephen's school days, he kept his word to his father. He always did his lessons first, before he played any music, or studied it, or wrote it. His school records were always good. As a reward at one time, he was allowed to have music lessons from Henry Kleber in Pittsburgh—the man who had given him his first flute.

That was the only formal music training that Stephen Foster had. But the lack of training did not keep him from becoming, at last, what he had always wanted to be: a full-time musician! But there were arguments and struggles before that time came.

Before Stephen was fifteen years old, his first song was published. "Open Thy Lattice, Love" is one of the Foster songs still sung with pleasure today.

Stephen Foster wrote more than three hundred published songs after that first one. In many, many of these, he was inspired by the Negro music he loved or by his memories of the South. Other American tunes and rhythms inspired him, too, so that people have called him "America's Folk Singer." His music did speak for the young country that was growing up in the early 1800's.

For a while after he finished school, Stephen tried dutifully to work at a bookkeeping job his parents urged him to take. Never did he neglect it, but he found ways for it to help him write music. He would go to the docks to make lists of goods coming by boat for his firm. And there he would listen, as he worked, to the songs the workmen sang. It was never difficult for him to find inspiration for a new song of his own.

He wrote many songs for minstrel singers who performed in his town. More and more people began to know the songs of Stephen Foster. At last he was able to devote all his time to music.

Today most Americans as well as people around the world know Stephen Foster's songs. You have probably sung some of them many times: "My Old Kentucky Home," "Old Black Joe," "Uncle Ned,"

"Camptown Races," "Jeannie with the Light Brown Hair." They are easy to sing and easy to remember, these lovely songs by a truly American composer.

DEEMS TAYLOR

Deems Taylor was always wondering. He wondered about everything he saw and everything he heard of. Back in the year 1892, when Deems was just starting to school in New York City, there were so many things for a curious boy to think about.

Deems wondered about the owners of the horse-drawn wagons and buses and carriages he saw on the busy city streets. He wondered if the iceman who delivered ice from a wagon ever stole a cool sliver of ice to eat, the way the city's children did.

Across from the Taylor home was a piano factory that Deems often wondered about. It seemed funny that beautiful-sounding pianos were made in factories, just as unbeautiful things were.

"Deems in Wonderingland" was what Mr. Taylor called his son. Then Deems wondered why his wise, schoolteacher father didn't know the right word was "Wonderland," not "Wonderingland."

"It's from *Alice in Wonderland*, Father," the little boy tried to explain. "You know, the funny book you read to me, about Alice!"

Mr. Taylor had laughed as he looked at Deem's serious little face. "For you, son, it is 'Wonderingland,' " he said. "Because you are always wondering."

Deems was interested in so many things that he did not think much about music until he was almost seven years old. He had always enjoyed listening to music at home, but he hadn't really *wondered* about it.

Then one day, he heard his mother singing while his father played the piano, and Deems stopped what he was doing to listen. He knew the words and music to that song, because it was his mother's favorite and she sang it often.

"In the gloaming, O my darling,
When the lights are soft and low . . ."

Deems stood in the doorway between dining room and parlor, munching cookies in time to the music. "In the Gloaming" was a lovely song, he thought. He began to wonder about it.

"Wonder how you write a song," Deems thought suddenly. The idea interested him. "Hmm, I just wonder."

With a piece of cookie halfway to his mouth,

Deems was lost in his thoughts. His parents had finished the song, and were looking at him with amused smiles. Then his Mother burst out laughing at him. She came to the doorway to give him a hug. "What are you thinking about, Deems? I mean, about what are you wondering now?"

"About music," said Deems, with his mouth full of cookie crumbs, "music and how you go about writing songs and things like that."

"Hmm. We knew you were wondering about something," said Mr. Taylor. "You had that 'Deems in Wonderingland' look."

Deems was still wondering how one would go about writing a song. "That was beautiful," he said. "Sing it again, and let me watch what you do when you play, Papa." Deems's parents looked at each other questioningly. This was a new and interesting kind of curiosity from the boy.

"All right," said Mr. Taylor. "Are you ready, my dear?"

Mrs. Taylor smiled, cleared her throat, and her husband began to play the introduction to the song.

This time, Deems sat on a low stool so that he could watch his father's hands and feet as he played.

"They go together, in a way," he thought. "I wonder how he can work the pedals with his feet and still keep in time with his fingers when they touch the different keys at different times. And I wonder why some keys are black and some white. And why aren't there as many black ones as white ones?"

He watched and listened and wondered.

"There," said his father when the song was over. "Did that help your wondering?"

"Y-yes," said Deems a bit uncertainly. "Some. But it made me wonder about a lot more things . . . Why you played in some places where Mama didn't sing. And why that little dollar sign is on those lines up above and the big C made backwards is on the lines below. And lots of things about the keys. And I wondered if I could write some songs if I could find out about all those things."

"I wonder, I wonder!" said Mr. Taylor, laughing. "I wonder if you would like me to read to you while Mama gets us some supper."

"Yes!" cried Deems, forgetting about music for a while. "Can we go on with *Alice Through the Looking Glass?*"

That was his favorite book at the moment. He loved the fun in it, and the many droll characters, and he never tired of hearing the story.

During supper, Deems began to think about songs again. Suddenly he announced, "I'm going to write a song book."

"Oh," said his mother. "Why, that's fine, Deems.

And perhaps I shall be allowed to sing the songs?"

"They probably won't be good enough—not at first, anyway," said Deems.

Mr. Taylor smiled approvingly. "Now that remark shows good sense and good logic. What kind of song book is this to be, my son?"

"Songs about all kinds of things," Deems answered thoughtfully. "There will be a song about being good, a song about being bad, a happy one, a sad one, just everything. I wonder if I can learn how to write down the notes on those music lines in time."

"Oh, you have a time limit?" his father asked, smiling again. But he sobered when he saw the warning look on Mrs. Taylor's face. "He is serious," her look meant, and he saw he must stop teasing.

"Well," he said sincerely, "what is the time limit? Perhaps I can help you to meet it."

"My birthday," said Deems. "It's a long way off, three whole months, but there's an awful lot I have to learn. All about the notes and lines and that dollar sign and stuff. I wonder if I can do it."

"And don't forget school, too," reminded Mrs. Taylor. "First-grade boys have to spend some time on their school work."

"Oh, but that's easy, Mama," Deems said. "The teacher told us all the things we would study, and I've already done that right here at home."

"What things?" asked Mr. Taylor. Since he was a teacher himself, he was especially interested.

"We learn the alphabet, and how to read, and how to write our name and address and age—all that. You've already taught me those things. And then teacher said we would draw, and sing and learn the notes on the scale. That might help me some in writing songs, but not so much as you and Mama can help. Teacher can't sing worth a penny."

Mr. and Mrs. Taylor both laughed this time.

"Now how in the world do you know she can't?" asked Deem's mother.

"Because," said Deems. "She sang, to show us what we'll sing to each other when the bell rings in the morning.

"Good morning to you-oo," Deems sang.
"Good morning to you-oo-oo!
"Good morning, dear children,
"Good morning to you!"

He made a face and put his fingers in his ears. "It was awful, and she sang off key. She knew it though."

"Well, I think that was very intelligent of her, and courageous too," said Mrs. Taylor. "If she knows pitch and can't quite make it, she is far better off than thinking she knows it. In that case, some of the children would have a bad start in music, especially those who really need help."

Deems said, "I wonder though, if she *ought* to sing the greeting in the morning, if she can't sing. I wonder if it wouldn't be better just to say it."

"You are quite right in wondering that," said his father. "I'm glad to know you have a good ear for music, son. Now, if you have finished eating, let's have our first lesson."

That was the beginning of lessons in music for Deems Taylor. Between lessons, he worked on his book of songs with enthusiasm and energy. The book was finished by his seventh birthday, as he had planned, and he presented it to his father and mother gleefully.

"Here it is! Here it is! See, Papa! Mama! My book of songs is finished!

"I am looking," said Mama with a happy smile. "And I'm so proud! Oh, it has a title. Look, Papa."

"Yes, I see," answered Mr. Taylor. "'Musical Gems.' Good title. Yes, this is very nice."

The leaves of the song book were tied together, and there was a pretty cover made of colored paper. Deems was proud of every part of his work.

"Isn't the cover pretty, Papa?" he demanded.

"It is indeed, Deems. But of course, you can't always tell a book by its cover."

"Tell it what?" asked Deems, looking up quickly with his wondering eyes. "Tell it what, Papa?"

"No, no," said his father, a bit startled. "I did not mean you tell the book something. That phrase means that you cannot tell what a book is like if you look only at its cover and not at what is inside. So suppose we look at the songs, now. Or better still, hear them."

Deems took the book eagerly and hurried to the piano. "Let me play some for you! Of course," he said, "you could play them much better, but I just want to see how well I can do it."

So he played a happy song and a sad song from his own songbook.

His parents thought the music was as good as the book was good-looking. "They are beautiful little songs," said Mrs. Taylor. "I am going to learn them at once. I shall love singing them! Think of my seven-year-old-son—No! Not even seven, until to-morrow! Think of his writing a book of songs! I am a very proud mother."

"And I am proud, too, Deems," said Mr. Taylor, looking at the little book with admiration. "This book represents many good things. It means that patience, imagination, good common sense, study, and no little talent all got together and went to work. We must keep this book. It will be a good lesson to all of us when the going gets hard and we feel like giving up."

Deems was happy as a lark. "I'm glad you really like it!" he said. "I wonder what kind of a song I ought to write next."

But there were so many interesting things in his life that Deems could not possibly think about music all of the time. One of the most exciting things, full of wonder, was his trip to the World's Fair in Chicago, in the summer of 1893.

Deems wondered about everything on the train from New York to Chicago. Was there ever such a long train with so many cars? Were all the hundreds of people on the train going to the Fair, too? Where did you eat on a train? Where did you sleep? Did you have to curl up on the benches?

He wondered most about sleeping. From what he saw before dinner, he could not understand how people would go to bed on the train. Yet his mother told him it was quite possible. "Just wait and see, Deems," she said. "We will go to bed after dinner."

Deems was sleepy before dinner was over, partly because he ate so much. But he was determined to stay wide awake and see what happened.

Mr. and Mrs. Taylor and Deems walked back through the train from the dining car to the car where their seats were.

"Here it is," said Mr. Taylor, looking at the number of a car as he opened its door.

Deems looked at his father, astonished.

"Oh, no, Papa!" he said. "This couldn't be it. Remember, it had benches on each side of the aisle, and this car just has long green curtains. I wonder why."

"The answer is behind the long green curtains, son," said Mr. Taylor, pleased at his little son's great interest in everything. Certainly no one could get more pleasure or learn more from a long journey and a world's fair than Deems could.

Quietly the Taylors walked through the dark car.

"See the numbers on the curtains?" Mr. Taylor whispered to Deems.

"Yes, but—" Deems hesitated. "But I wonder . . ."

"I know," answered his father.

From somewhere behind a green curtain, a loud whisper hissed, "Shhh!" From another direction came a gruff voice: "Quiet, please!"

"That is what it said on a sign when we came in," Deems whispered excitedly. " 'Quiet Please.' I was wondering why."

"Because it is time to go to bed. Now, Deems, our number for our 'benches', as you call them, was seven, wasn't it?"

"Yes, Papa. I remember, because I'm that old."

Mrs. Taylor giggled, like a little girl. Her family turned and scolded her, "Shhh! Quiet, please!"

"All right," said Papa softly. "Now, here we are at Number 7, so we have the right to push aside the curtains. There! See?"

"It's beds!" shouted Deems, forgetting to whisper. "SHHHHH!" "SHHHHH!" came from several places in the car. But there was some laughing, too. After all, it was not very late.

"What happens now," asked Deems, "with one bed upstairs and one bed downstairs? Could I sleep up above?"

"He might fall out," whispered his mother.

"He couldn't, with those strong, wide straps," Mr. Taylor answered. "It's much more fun up above. You know, dear, with the ladder and the little hammock for his clothes."

"Yes, of course," whispered Mrs. Taylor. "All right, Deems, up you go!"

"Mama is getting excited again," Mr. Taylor said to Deems. "She forgets we must wash up first. You come with me, son, and if you like, you can get into your night shirt in the wash room. Or, if you'd rather, you can do it doubled up in the upper berth."

"They call it upper berth and lower berth, Papa?"

Papa nodded, and Deems grinned with satisfaction. "Well, I would like to change in the wash room on the way to Chicago, and in the upper berth doubled up, on the way home!"

Everything was wonderful and exciting to Deems, not just on that trip, but all through the years of his growing up. Sometimes he said, "I simply don't know what I like the best or what I want to do most. I wish I could do everything when I grow up. What shall I do, I wonder?"

His father advised him, "Do for now exactly what you are doing. Enjoy and make use of every minute as it comes along. But always remember this, son. Whatever you do—now or any time—if you do it well, it will help you know for sure what you want most to do when you're grown."

At school the teachers were always interested in Deems. They liked his excitement about everything that happened, and they especially enjoyed his interest in music, which they encouraged every day. The music teacher liked his songs and the way he played the piano.

"Deems," she said one day, "you so often play original things on the piano. The children need music, and some of them seem unable to take an interest in the piano or violin. They have a foolish idea that it is 'sissy,' or something of that sort. Why don't you learn to play something you can carry around and have it with you any place you go? Think how much it would mean to the other children. You would enjoy it, too."

"Y-yes," said Deems. "Well, maybe. Maybe a harmonica?"

"Fine," said the teacher, "Yes, that is a very good idea."

"The only thing is," said Deems thoughtfully, "I have to earn the money to buy it. I can't ask Papa and Mama for extras like that. And I don't know how I can earn any money while I'm going to school. Unless . . ."

He remembered something interesting about *St. Nicholas Magazine*. That popular children's magazine had a contest each month. If a child wrote a poem good enough, he could win ten dollars. That much money would buy several harmonicas.

So Deems began to work on his poem. He became so interested and excited that without meaning to do it, he made a song of it. He called the song, "Going to Wonderland."

The verse for the song was good, and the music was very good. But it did not win the ten-dollar prize from the magazine. However, Deems did manage to earn what he needed for a harmonica.

The song that didn't win the prize did receive notice, though. A letter came from *St. Nicholas Magazine*. The editors said they liked what he had written very much, and they awarded him a silver badge of honor for his work.

Deems was delighted, and proud of the silver badge. He looked at it, and began to wonder seriously about music.

"Mama, I don't think I could ever be a great musician," he said. "But would it cost too much to study? I mean, is there any way I could take some real music lessons?"

"Of course you can," Mrs. Taylor said. "Papa will be glad. He has not time himself to teach you properly any more, but he has friends who are music teachers. We'll see about it at once."

So Deems Taylor began to study music. He knew how good music should sound, and he thought his own music was not good.

"I haven't enough talent," he often said. "Whatever you are, you ought to be really good at it. Good enough for people to enjoy what you do."

For a while, Deems worked in a piano factory. Then he spent a year working in the office of some publishers. All this time he also went to school, worked in boys' camps and attended extra classes in night school. Always he was curious, "wondering why" and finding out!

When he went to college, music claimed him again. There was no one else to write the college musical, so Deems wrote it. Victor Herbert, one of the best of all light opera composers, came to the show. Afterward, Mr. Herbert went to see the young man who had written it.

"I saw you, sir," said Deems. "I wondered if it really was you, the great Victor Herbert. I certainly hope you didn't think the show was too bad!"

"I did not," said Victor Herbert, with a smile. "I certainly did not. My boy, you have talent, a great deal of it. But you know nothing of harmony, do you?"

"No, sir," said Deems. "I have really never studied, you see."

"I do not see," answered Victor Herbert. "I do not see how you could write such music without having studied! That you had not studied harmony, yes, that I could tell; to write music without studying harmony is to write a poem without learning how to read. I knew you could read music, and I am sure you can play it. And now, my boy, you must study harmony, composition, all you can. You have a talent. It must not be wasted."

"Thank you, sir," said Deems, "thank you."

"I wonder what Father will say to this," he thought. "I had better tell him and find out."

Mr. Taylor was delighted.

"That is actually how I feel, myself!" he said happily. "However, I had no wish to impose my opinion on you, Deems. You have too many interests for me to interfere. But Victor Herbert is an expert, and I hope with all my heart you take his advice. Try in every way you can find to earn the money to do what you must do to become a musician.

"First of all," Mr. Taylor decided, "I shall lend you every penny of my savings. I know you would not take the money otherwise, but as a loan, which some day you shall repay, you must take it. For my sake and your Mother's, Deems, as well as your own. Then, try out for musical prizes. New York seems full of them! Find out about them. Good luck, son, and God bless you."

Deems got busy. With such encouragement, he felt he must and could do anything.

He heard about the plan of the National Federation of Music Clubs to give a prize scholarship for the best symphonic poem submitted by a student.

"Symphonic poem," thought Deems, "symphonic poem. That means I must write music for a whole orchestra, music for a poem. I hope I do better than I did on the *St. Nicholas* poem! Still, I did win a silver medal that time."

Deems Taylor wrote his first symphonic poem, "The Siren Song," for that contest, and won the scholarship. Then, he was filled with hope and confidence. He worked unendingly at his music after that.

"I guess I'm about the luckiest person in the world," he said. "I know I worked hard for this scholarship prize. But I feel lucky just the same. Now I hope I can always write music that people will like."

That is what Deems Taylor always did. Besides being a composer, he became a famous critic and commentator. He spent many years speaking about music on the radio and writing about it in newspapers, magazines and books.

His own music includes works for orchestra, songs, and operas. One of his orchestral works is *Alice Through the Looking Glass*. He must have enjoyed writing the music for *Alice*, the story he loved so much when he was a child. Anyone who has heard the pieces can never forget the marvelous musical pictures of the Knight, the White Rabbit, the Garden of Live Flowers and the Jabberwocky.

So the little boy who wondered grew up to be a man with many talents, who has written much beautiful music that people really like. He was "good enough," after all. Everyone who listens to music by Deems Taylor knows that. When you hear his music, you will feel in it Deems Taylor's belief in the goodness of people and the beauty and excitement of life. Is it not a great achievement—expressing such feelings in music?

Opera

JEROME KERN

Jerome Kern is a name you will hear whenever American music is talked about. His songs are songs you will hear, too. They are loved and sung all over America. Almost everything Jerome Kern wrote was popular from its first playing. Perhaps the most popular of his songs is "Smoke Gets in Your Eyes." Maybe you already know that one. If Kern had not written any other music, he would be remembered for "Smoke Gets in Your Eyes."

Jerome Kern was born in New York City in 1885. He lived in a pleasant, happy home, and he learned to like music from the time he was born. His mother loved to play and sing. The boy who lived next door practiced every day, too. By the time Jerome was three years old, he liked music so much that he missed it when the neighbor boy did not practice.

When Mrs. Kern played the piano or sang, she noticed that Jerome stayed happily quiet.

"Jerome, you like the music, don't you?" she often asked.

"Yes, Mother!"

Mrs. Kern was pleased. She knew how much pleasure music could give. One day she said to the little boy, "How would you like to go to an opera, and hear beautiful music sung on a big stage? All the actors will sing what they wish to say, instead of speaking, as they do in a play."

"I would like that!" said Jerome. "Will there be a piano, too? Will someone play the piano like you?"

"Maybe," said his mother. "But there will be a big orchestra, for sure."

"What's an or—Or-ches-tra?"

His mother described the many instruments of the orchestra. "They all play together," she said. "Rows of violins and violas, cellos, a harp, drums, horns, flutes—all sorts of musical instruments playing together! With an opera you will always find big orchestras."

Jerome was more interested than before, and went eagerly with his mother to the opera.

He was only four years old, and it was an adventure he never forgot. He used to tell of it in later years, after he was grown and famous. He remembered it because it was so important to his life, after that day.

When the first notes of melody were sung by the actors in the opera, Jerome whispered loudly, "Mother, it's so pretty! I like it!"

But from that moment on, he kept quiet. He did not grow restless, or tired of listening to the music. He was perfectly happy. Even on the way home, he did not talk. He was busy remembering what he had seen and how the music sounded.

When he reached home, he broke his silence by singing his father a song from the opera.

"Isn't that a pretty song, Father?" he said. "I love that music. Just listen!" He sang the air again.

"Yes, it is very beautiful," his father agreed. "When did you learn this song, Jerome?"

"This afternoon, Father," Jerome said, excitedly. "At the opera. It was wonderful! I won't ever forget it."

Mr. Kern laughed then. "Come now, Jerome, you could never have learned that song just from hearing it once, this afternoon. You must have heard it somewhere else, before. Isn't that right, Mother?"

Mrs. Kern said, "No, my dear, I am afraid you are wrong. I'm quite sure the child has never heard the song before. I couldn't believe my ears, myself, when I heard him just now. Why, he must be a genius," she added proudly.

"A genius!" Mr. Kern looked very serious. He

stroked his chin thoughtfully. "A genius! Well, perhaps we cannot tell about that quite so soon! However, I must admit he may be a musical prodigy, my dear. You are a most excellent musician, yourself. Why don't you give Jerome a few music lessons, and see what happens?"

"I am not sure it would be wise," said Mrs. Kern, doubtfully. "After all, the child is only four years old."

Suddenly Jerome himself spoke up.

"Please, please, oh please, Mama, let me take the lessons! Then I can play the piano, too. I can be like you and the boy next door! Let me learn how to play the music, Mama. I want to play—not just listen! Please!"

His parents smiled at such an outburst.

"I am glad," said Mama, "very glad you feel that way. But I think we should wait until you are a little older, Jerome. Now, you must have plenty of fresh air and sunshine so you will grow to be strong and healthy. When you are big enough to reach the keys and the pedals and read the music all at the same time, I will teach you."

Jerome Kern never allowed his mother to forget that promise. But he played the best he could without lessons. He picked out scales on the piano himself, and played them every day. Then he found a melody he liked and played it with one finger. Some melodies he had heard; others he made up himself.

The day of Jerome's fifth birthday he woke up with a song in his heart—for he felt quite grown-up at last.

"I'm five years old! It's my birthday and I'm five years old! Now I can have music lessons. I must be old enough, Mother."

"Yes, dear. Happy birthday!" His mother smiled at his excitement. "We're going downtown today, you and I."

"Will we ride in the horse-car, Mother? Will we?"

"Yes, dear."

When Jerome went with his mother that morning on a big, lumbering, horse-car bus, he felt very grown-up indeed. The conductor seemed to think Jerome looked grown-up, too. When he came for the tickets, he looked at the little boy sitting up so straight and asked, "How old is the child, Madam, if you please?"

"Four," said Jerome's mother absently. "Four years old."

"No, Mother—not now!" cried Jerome. "I am five years old today." Jerome looked at the conductor proudly. "This is my birthday. I have to pay, now that I am five, don't I, Mama?"

"Of course you do. I'm sorry, I quite forgot."

Jerome's mother smiled at the conductor. "He's only been five a short time. Truly, I forgot."

"Didn't you forget something else, Mama?" asked Jerome. "Did you forget you promised to start giving me music lessons when I was more grown-up?"

Nothing could make Jerome forget about music, that was easy to see!

"I had almost forgotten," said Mrs. Kern. "You reminded me just in time. Yes, you have waited long enough, and we shall start the lessons today."

So for nearly a year Jerome worked and studied with his mother. But the work was simple and easy for him. He began to listen more carefully to the boy next door. Each evening when Jerome went to bed, he could see his neighbor practicing. Sometimes he watched the boy's lessons. Jerome would stand up on his bed and watch and listen eagerly, whenever he saw the music teacher next door.

"If other boys can take music lessons from regular music teachers," he thought, "and practice every day to play music like that, I ought to do it, too! When I'm six years old, I ought to have regular lessons with a regular teacher."

On his sixth birthday, it seemed to Jerome that unless he could start a real study of music, his heart would be broken. Early in the morning that day, shouting, he woke up everyone in the house.

"I'm six years old today! I'm six years old today. I'm getting grown-up. And I must have music lessons. Other boys do. Why can't I? If I have to sell newspapers or something to pay for them, I will. I have to have music lessons, now!"

"Goodness, Jerome!" said his mother anxiously. "Maybe I haven't taken you quite seriously enough. But you shall have your wish, without selling papers, because your father and I are giving you a very special present for your birthday—a whole series of music lessons with Miss Hirschfield. She's a very good teacher."

At last, real music lessons—with a real teacher!

"When do I begin?" the boy demanded.

"Today," said his mother. "Miss Hirschfield is coming this afternoon."

So Jerome began to take lessons that very day. He had a lesson almost every day, after that. Even with that much study, he often thought he would never make up the time he had lost *before* he was six years old.

From that time on, Jerome Kern never forgot the dream in his heart of learning to know music, of being able to make songs of the melodies he heard in the world about him. When he was only twelve years old, he played his own music to the words of popular songs, trying to make the songs sound better. He was never satisfied with his work. He was always looking for something better.

"I like what they call popular music," he thought. "It has something different in tempo and mood that I like. But there is something wrong. The words are not good enough or the tunes are not good enough, or both. Some day I will write words and music for popular songs that will be *good* songs, with the right words to the right music. And all over America people will sing my songs. Some day . . ."

That is really the way Jerome Kern felt when he was young. He often thought of it and spoke of it to others whenever music was discussed.

As the years passed, he did just as he had planned. He was determined to make his dream come true, and it did.

Jerome Kern stands with other American composers whose music makes a new chapter in American history. His music—popular music that is good music, too—truly expresses the spirit of a lively and growing America.

GEORGE GERSHWIN

Clattering horse-drawn wagons! Sputtering, gasping motor cars with their loud horns! Thundering elevated trains, clanging trolleys, millions of footsteps of millions of people, all day long! That was the song of the city, New York City in 1905. That was the song little George Gershwin heard whenever he played on the city's streets.

He was six-going-on-seven that year of 1905, and full of energy. When he went down the street, he didn't walk—he ran, just for the fun of it. He added a whoop and a shout of his own to the sounds of the street. He stopped to investigate nearly everything he saw. So sometimes he was slow getting home, even when he knew he should hurry.

One summer afternoon, when George should have been home to help the family get ready to move, he was standing on a street corner instead. He was listening eagerly to music that came from an old phonograph in a store. This music was different from any he'd heard before. It had jumps in it. It wasn't a jazz rhythm, exactly. There was just a "surprise beat" now and then.

"That's good," George Gershwin thought as he listened. "That funny jump beat—I like it."

As he went home after the music stopped, he still heard the rhythm in his head. Rhythm was what he liked best about music.

But there were many things, in those days, that George liked much more than any kind of music. He liked to play ball and to roller skate. He liked active games that let him get rid of some of his energy.

"George, where have you been?" His brother Ira hailed him. "Mother wants you! We must all help if we're to get moved tonight."

George raced up the stairs of the apartment house, burst into the little apartment. He wrestled Ira across the living room to a closet. Then he jumped high enough to reach an old cap on the closet shelf. Laughing, he threw the cap over Ira's head toward the box that was being packed.

"I'll pack! I'll pack!" he shouted.

The first cap was followed by more caps, then sweaters and overalls, bundled into bulky balls. George threw everything from the closet into the box. Ira caught the spirit and began to pack that way, too.

It was impossible to be around George for long and feel unhappy. His joy of life and his sense of fun were contagious. Everyone always felt better when George was around.

His busy mother and father had to laugh at him, even on moving day. He really did get his work done, they knew.

He marched around the apartment like a band leader, making a game out of everything he did. In spite of all the confusion, the Gershwins were ready to go when the time came. And the next night, the family slept in the new home on Seventh Street, far downtown.

After the boys started to their new school, George was on the lower grades' ball team and hockey team. Soon he was the roller-skating champion of Seventh Street. It was a gay, happy, exciting life, and to George everything was fun except work and school.

Ira was different. He seemed to enjoy books and studies as much as George disliked them. It was not long before George's teacher began to call Ira in once a week.

"Ira, can't you do something to help George?" she would say. "He studies just enough to pass. But he is so bright, he could learn a lot more than he does. And his deportment is dreadful! Won't you talk to him?"

"Yes, ma'am." Ira was always embarrassed at these talks with the teacher. He tried to defend his little brother. "George is just so full of pep, ma'am. It makes him seem a little wild. He's kind, though. He wouldn't hurt Mother and Father for anything. He just has to work off steam, I guess."

Then Ira would go home and, as he had promised, "talk" to George.

"Please, George," he said, "I wish you'd try to pay attention in school, and study when you're supposed to, and not get the lowest grade in deportment for the whole class! Please try. Then I won't have to see your teacher every week!"

George was always sorry, and always thinking he would do better. "I try, Ira, really I try. But—so many things are running around in my head. Ideas I have to work out. There are so many things I must do."

"Yes, I know, George. But try again, will you?"

The boys always seemed to understand and enjoy each other. Even though they were so different, they liked to be together and always had fun together.

One of George's big ideas that he actually worked out was to skate from Seventh Street to Central Park and back. He wasn't such a little boy, then; he was ten by that time. But still, all the way up and back was more than a hundred blocks, not an easy journey. George and his friends on Seventh Street didn't know how long the trip would take, but they thought they could do it between breakfast and suppertime.

"Send me a postcard!" said Ira. He had no wish to go along. But he would cheer for George, just the same.

Central Park seemed to get farther and farther away as George and the other boys skated along. One by one the boys turned back, roller skates strapped across their shoulders instead of on their shoes. Finally, all of them had given up except George. He lifted his chin, clenched his fists, and skated. He skated slowly, on and on and on.

Grimly, he muttered to himself: "I'm ten years old and I'm not a quitter and I'm not a sissy. I started this thing and I'll finish it if it's the last thing I ever do."

When at last Seventh Street came in sight, there was Ira, looking anxious and worried. But George's spirits lifted. He felt like singing. He had made it!

"Hey! Ira! Look out! I can't stop! Look out, Ira, or I'll bump into you!"

Down went both boys, a tangle of arms and legs and roller skates on the sidewalk.

"Ira, I told you to look out!"

Ira helped his younger brother to his feet. "I'm sorry, George, but I was so glad to see you and so surprised I just couldn't move."

"Well, that's that," said George ruefully. "I skated all the way, but the last crossing! All the way to Central Park and back. And then I have to crash and spoil the whole thing."

"What are you talking about?" said Ira. "You made it! You're the only one. That's all that counts. It wasn't your fault I got in the way. You're the real champ!"

George was quickly comforted by his big brother. Suddenly he felt fine, not even tired any more.

"Hurray!" he shouted, throwing his cap in the air. Then he stared up at the third-floor apartment.

"Ira, look! What's that fellow doing? What is that thing?"

"Oh, you mean the pulley and the piano! I forgot to tell you," Ira said. "I have to take piano lessons. Mother said so. So, that's our new piano."

"Ours!" George looked up in wondering disbelief. "Look at that! See how it goes up to the third floor, outside the building. I hope that rope doesn't break."

The rope didn't break. The piano was carefully pulled in through the window.

George shouted excitedly, "Come on, Ira! Beat you up the stairs!"

On the third floor landing, he stopped and said, "A piano. A real piano." He said it again when he rushed into the living room and saw the piano sitting there.

"Of course it's a piano," said Ira. "What is the matter with you, George? Haven't you ever seen a piano before?"

"Not here. Not right here in this room, in our own house. I want to play something on it."

Ira asked incredulously, "How can you play the piano without lessons? Don't be so silly."

"I can play the scale," said George soberly. "Anyone can do that."

He seemed to forget Ira was there. He sat down on the piano stool as though he had done it a thousand times before, and played the scale, first with one hand, then with both hands. He tried a few notes of a piece that sounded familiar to Ira. Then, firmly and surely and remarkably well, he began the piece again. It was "Alexander's Ragtime Band," a "hit song" of the day.

For the first time, it was Ira who shouted, Ira who was excited. "That's 'Alexander's Ragtime Band!' George Gershwin! When did you learn how to play the piano?"

"I don't know, Ira," said George. "I mean, I didn't know I could play that piece. I've tried to play once in a while at someone else's house, if there was a piano. I like the sound of a piano. I like trying to play."

He seemed surprised at himself, almost as surprised as Ira was. "You know, I'd like to take lessons. I never thought of that before."

Up he jumped, running to the kitchen door and shouting, "Mother! Where are you? Mother!"

"Goodness, George! What is the matter?" His mother came into the living room with a worried look on her face. "Oh, thank goodness you're all right! I thought you were hurt."

"I'm fine. But I want to take piano lessons, too, along with Ira. I have to! I have to learn how to play—really play, I mean."

It was his mother's turn to be surprised. "Why, George, when would you practice? It's all I can do to get you to finish your homework after school. No, dear, Ira is the student in the family. You would never have the patience to sit down and practice every day. You'd be outside roller skating or playing baseball."

"I would practice, Mother, I would." George looked so desperate his mother patted him gently on the shoulder.

"Oh, Mother, this is different!" he said. "I'll work. I promise. Please."

"George, don't get so excited. You might take a few lessons and if you really practice . . . well, then we'll see."

So when he was ten years old, George Gershwin had his first music lessons. After a few weeks with a neighborhood teacher, he was accepted by a fine musician, Charles Hambritzer. Mr. Hambritzer was impressed with George's talent. He began to think that the boy was a genius. But he did not approve of George's fondness for modern music, for jazz. That would be all right later, after George had a good grounding in classical music. So he insisted that the boy study and practice the works of the masters.

George didn't mind. He liked the music of Bach, Chopin, Liszt and Debussy, and practiced it eagerly.

But then he practiced everything with enthusiasm, and no one ever had to tell him to practice. He could not leave the piano.

One day, just a few months after George had begun studying, he had a surprise for Mr. Hambritzer.

"Excuse me, sir," he said, "there's something I want to ask you. That is, well, I wrote a song. The music, I mean. Ira wrote the words, and *they're* fine but something is wrong with the music. I thought maybe you could tell me what it is."

"Of course, George, of course," said Mr. Hambritzer warmly. "Let's hear it."

George began to play, singing and moving his whole body in rhythm.

When he finished, he looked up anxiously. "Something is wrong," he said. "It's at the end. What's the matter with the end of it, Mr. Hambritzer? Do you know?"

"Yes. I know," answered the teacher with an amused smile. Then when he saw how serious George looked and how troubled he was, he became serious, too. "Look, my boy, what is wrong is this: You have started your song in the key of C and you have finished it in the key of A. Your musical ear knows this is wrong. But your musical mind cannot explain why because it does not know the rules of harmony and composition."

George looked puzzled. "Harmony and composition?"

"You cannot expect to write music," Mr. Hambritzer told him, "without knowledge of harmony and composition. A composer must know and understand these things. He must know how music is created. There are rules, just as there are rules for doing arithmetic problems. But learning them takes time, hard work and study. And this you do not like, though you do work well when it comes to practicing the piano."

"Harmony and composition," said George

thoughtfully. "All right. If I have to learn harmony and composition to write music, I'll learn it. Because I have to write music. I can't keep hearing it in all the noises every place without putting it down so I can play it."

The next time George played one of his own compositions, he played it from his own manuscript, correctly written.

Ira could hardly believe his eyes when he saw it. "Oh," he whispered softly. "You have changed, George. Why, if anybody had ever told me you would study hard enough and long enough to learn harmony and composition, I would have laughed in his face! Look at you. A composer! All you ever thought about before you saw that piano was roller skating and baseball. This looks like real music. What is it?"

"It's a tango, Ira. It's correct as far as the writing goes. That's what Mr. Hambritzer said. But that doesn't mean a thing if it doesn't have feeling . . . You know what I mean. Listen and tell me what you think of it.

George played that tango with his fingers, his feet, his head, his whole body. Ira found himself moving to the rhythm of the tango. When George finished playing he looked anxiously at the big brother he loved and admired so much.

"Well," he asked, "what do you think? It is all right, Ira?"

"All right?" said Ira excitedly. "It's great! It's wonderful! You could dance to it!"

By the time George was in his early teens, he was wishing for a job in the music business. He wondered what he might do, while he was still going to school. He thought of something that made his dark eyes light up.

"Ira," he said, "I'd like to get a job this summer song-plugging in a publishing house on Tin Pan Alley. You know, where people bring in songs to sell, and someone plays them to get people to buy them? That's a good way to learn about popular music. Mr. Hambritzer said he wouldn't mind too much, if I keep on playing Bach, too!"

"Well," said Ira, "why don't you go ahead and try?"

"I will," said George solemnly. "I'll do it."

When school was out, he made an appointment at Remick's music publishing house. When the day came, he felt like running away before he went in the door. His knees were quaking. For once, George Gershwin was very quiet.

The manager looked up and grumbled crossly when he saw George. "Well, what is it? What do you want, youngster?"

"I'm the boy who wrote to ask for an appointment about a job," said George. "I thought you said you would see me today."

"Oh no!" groaned the manager. "I said that to get rid of you. No jobs here. Don't need an errand boy. Don't need an office boy. What we need is a musician, a song-plugger. But try to find one!"

George looked at the upright piano in the corner, cleared his throat and managed to find his voice.

"Well, that's what I mean, sir. That's why I wanted to see you. I have a few songs, too. I can play the piano. And I do know something about song-writing. . . ."

George was embarrassed. This was the first job he had ever applied for, and he didn't know quite what to do or say. He stopped talking and moved toward the door. But the manager stopped him.

"Wait a minute, son. You play the piano, and you have a few songs of your own. So let's hear you. What are we waiting for? There's the piano, let's hear something."

"Yes, sir!" said George.

He sat down on the rickety piano stool, his big envelope of music forgotten. Nervously he wiped the perspiration off his face and hands.

He was scared but he played, as he always played, with his heart, his head, hands, feet, body and soul.

Then he was frightened and embarrassed again in the silence that followed his playing. Suddenly he made a dash for the door, apologizing as he went.

"Excuse me, Mr. Gimble. I'm sorry. I know it wasn't any good for the kind of work you want. Thank you, anyway. Good-by."

"Wait a minute!" At last the manager looked almost pleasant. "Who said I couldn't use you?" What's your name?"

"George, sir. George Gershwin."

Mr. Gimble nodded. "George Gershwin. Well, we don't need a composer, George, but we need a song-plugger. I never heard of one your age, but there's always a first time. Can you transpose to any key at sight?"

"Yes, sir."

"So far, so good," said Mr. Gimble. "You'll have to go to cafes at night some times, and to small towns around New York. The pay is fifteen dollars a week. Want to start Monday?"

"Yes, sir!"

Somehow George managed to nod his head and get out the door without stumbling. It was not easy.

There was a mixed reaction at home. Mr. and Mrs. Gershwin agreed the job would do for a summer, but no more than that. Ira knew the work would be more difficult than George realized. But he was proud of his young brother and he encouraged him.

Ira's understanding was all George needed. "What if I do have to play the piano eight or ten hours a day and sometimes in the evening! I'm glad of it," said George. "It's what I need to learn more about the music of show business. I can practice at Remick's, too."

George was right about that, but he soon realized that playing popular songs all day was a one-sided education. So every afternoon or evening that he had to himself, he went to concerts. He almost haunted the concert halls of the city.

It was after one concert that Ira came home to find George playing some music of Bach. It was difficult music, and Ira had never heard his brother play it before. He could tell, as he listened, that George did not even know anyone else was in the room.

When at last George stopped, Ira applauded softly. "That was fine!" he said. "How do you do it?"

"You know what, Ira? When I go to a concert, I listen. I mean, I listen with my ears, of course, but with—with my nerves, too—you know? I listen so hard I'm soaked in the music. Then I come straight home and see if I can play it myself. Sounds silly, doesn't it?"

Ira patted his brother on the shoulder. "Silly? No, it sounds very good! I couldn't have put it better myself."

When George Gershwin was not quite sixteen, he wrote the music for a song that was actually published. He was paid five dollars; the man who wrote the words got fifteen dollars! But George didn't mind the difference in fee. People liked his music enough to use it and pay for it, that was the important thing. And he had the thrill of seeing "Music by George Gershwin" on the cover of a popular song.

After that, he wrote and wrote. His music pleased the composer, Sigmund Romberg, and he was invited to write a song for a musical show with Romberg. He wrote other numbers for other musicals, and learned more about "show business." He decided he did not want to write what he called "Tin Pan Alley stuff," but good music for shows, "catchy tunes that really mean something," he said.

One day, George suddenly decided to stop song-plugging, and look for something else to do. Just what it would be, he did not know. But it had to be a position that would leave him time to practice, and to compose.

There were hard times and good. He worked as a theater pianist—and lost his place in the music right in the middle of the show. He played for popular singers. He worked for another music publishing house, which brought out three songs in one year with music by Gershwin.

Then came a big success. Al Jolson sang "Swanee" in a show, and suddenly, all over the country, people were singing George Gershwin's music. "Swanee" became the most popular song of the time. George Gershwin was on his way.

In 1924, less than fifteen years after his first music lesson, George was asked by the orchestra leader, Paul Whitman, to compose something for a jazz concert. *Rhapsody in Blue*, for piano and orchestra, was the result. *Rhapsody in Blue* proclaimed to all the world the genius of George Gershwin.

Later, describing how he felt about the *Rhapsody*, George said, "It's America, the big melting pot—the energy and vigor — the shows — the changing countryside. It's the city with its rush and its noise. America, young and exciting, and growing, growing—with all the people going, going, going!"

There was no lack of work or cheers for Gershwin after that historic jazz concert. He wrote music commissioned by the New York Philharmonic Orchestra. He wrote music for stage shows; music for famous solo performers. He wrote a great American opera, *Porgy and Bess*.

The music of George Gershwin expresses the character and personality of its composer, which may be one reason so many people like it. It is joyous music, and quite typical of America, as he wanted it to be.